Lambrakis and the Peace Movement

The Greek May of 1963

ΔΡΟΜΟΙ ΤΗΣ Ειρήνης

ΑΡΙΘΜΟΣ ΦΥΛΛΟΥ 66 — ΤΙΜΗ ΔΡΧ. 5

ΤΟ ΠΡΟΣΩΠΙΚΟ ΗΜΕΡΟΛΟΓΙΟ ΤΟΥ ΓΡΗΓΟΡΗ ΛΑΜΠΡΑΚΗ

ΕΠΑΝΕΚΔΟΣΗ
για τα 25χρονα
από τη δολοφονία του
ΓΡΗΓΟΡΗ ΛΑΜΠΡΑΚΗ
ΜΑΗΣ 1988 ΤΙΜΗ ΔΡΧ. 200

«ἀφιέρωμα στὸν Γρ. Λαμπράκη»

Grigoris Lambrakis and one of his three sons on the cover of Roads of Peace *in June 1963, a month after his assassination. The photo was used again for his 25th anniversary, in 1988.*

Lambrakis
and the
Peace Movement
The Greek May of 1963

PANOS TRIGAZIS

SPOKESMAN
Nottingham

First published in Greece in 2013
First published in English translation in 2014 by Spokesman
Russell House, Bulwell Lane,
Nottingham NG6 0BT, England
Phone: 0115 9708381   Fax: 01159420433
e-mail: elfeuro@compuserve.com
www.spokesmanbooks.com

ISBN 978 0 85124 833 2

A CIP Catalogue is available from the British Library

Printed in Nottingham by Russell Press Ltd. (www.russellpress.com)

Contents

Acronyms

AKE	Independent Peace Movement
AKEL	Progressive Party for the Working People
CCOSO	Co-ordinating Committee of Overseas Students Organisations
CND	Campaign for Nuclear Disarmament
COMECON	Council for Mutual Economic Assistance
CTBT	Comprehensive Nuclear-Test-Ban Treaty
CWC	Chemical Weapons Convention
DOKEP	International Olympic Centre for Peace and Culture
EAM	National Liberation Front
EDA	United Democratic Left
EDNE	United Democratic Youth of Greece
EEA	Association of Greek Athletes
EEC	European Economic Community
EEDYE	Greek Committee for International Détente and Peace, or Greek Peace Committee
EFEE	National Student Union of Greece
EKOF	National Students' Social Organisation
ELAS	National Popular Liberation Army
END	European Nuclear Disarmament
EPON	United Panhellenic Organization of Youth
ERE	National Radical Union
ESIEA	Union of Athens Daily Newspaper Journalists
INF	Intermediate Nuclear Forces
IPB	International Peace Bureau
IPPNW	International Physicians for the Prevention of Nuclear War
KEADEA	Movement for Peace, Human Rights and National Independence
KKE	Communist Party of Greece
LDG	League for Democracy in Greece
LDY	Lambrakis Democratic Youth
MAD	Mutually Assured Destruction
MAPAM	United Workers Party
MP	Member of Parliament
NATO	North Atlantic Treaty Organization
NTUA	National Technical University of Athens
PADOP	Observatory of International Organizations and Globalization
PAME	Pandemocratic Agrarian Front of Greece
PASOK	Panhellenic Socialist Movement
PLO	Palestine Liberation Organization
SALT	Strategic Arms Limitation Treaty

SEGAS	Hellenic Amateur Athletic Association
START	Strategic Arms Reduction Treaty
SYRIZA	The Coalition of Radical Left
TYPA	Health and Care Fund for Athletes
UN	United Nations
UNESCO	United Nations Educational, Scientific and Cultural Organization
USSR	Union of Soviet Socialist Republics
WPC	World Peace Counci

United Democratic Left (EDA)

Forewords

In the Hands of the People
Manolis Glezos

It has often been said that human history is a history of wars. But the opposite can also be said, which is that human history is a perpetual search for the ideal of peace, and a struggle in the pursuit of it. This can be seen in great works of world literature, and the works of major historians, philosophers and political thinkers. The timelessness and global repute of the ancient Greek tragedies are due to their anti-war and humanitarian messages.

In Greece, the peace cause took the form of an organised movement in the twentieth century. Its struggles were always interwoven with the growing movement of the Left and the people's struggle for democracy and national independence. The anti-fascist movement in Greece and Europe in the interwar period and during World War Two was at the same time a mass movement for peace and freedom.

It is not accidental that major figures of the anti-fascist struggle, such as Einstein, Picasso, and our own Nikos Karvounis and Petros Kokkalis, were prime movers in the international peace movement as well – nor is it accidental that hundreds of Greek resistance fighters in EAM-ELAS and EPON worked in the Greek peace movement that developed after the Civil War, and played a leading role in its growth. Among these resistance fighters were the pioneers Nikos Nikiforidis (Secretary of EPON in Pagrati) and Grigoris Lambrakis.

Grigoris Lambrakis was an exuberant personality, a courageous and ardent fighter for peace, democracy and social justice. We walked together in 1963 on the great march from the atomic weapons facility in Aldermaston to London, where we got to know each other, and I became a profound admirer of his passion for peace.

That visit to London (together with Leonidas Kyrkos and Spyros Linardatos) to take part in the Aldermaston march gave me an opportunity to meet the great British philosopher Bertrand Russell, leader of the British anti-nuclear movement and consistent supporter of the Greek people's struggle for democracy and national independence, as is shown clearly in this book.

We met Russell, then an elderly man, at his country place in Wales. Although he was well informed about the police state in Greece, he wanted to learn even more and to be equipped with more arguments in his struggle to stop 'the humiliation of the Greek nation' as he described it. The discussion revolved around issues of nuclear disarmament and how to defeat 'human folly'. His calm manner and the depth and breadth of his thinking impressed me. I fully understood that the special nature of Bertrand Russell lay in the fact that his scholarly presence and activity aimed not to push himself forward as a leader, but to raise public awareness to a movement of collective self-knowledge, so that the fate of humankind would reside solely in the hands of the people.

I am very happy that my friend and comrade Panos Trigazis – a man with profound knowledge of this subject from both the national and international viewpoint – has chosen to write about Grigoris Lambrakis and the peace movement. The 50-year chronicle of the peace movement in this book is extremely interesting, a source of his ideas and valuable experiences in the development of today's struggles for peace and democracy by the Left, the Greek people and youth. This book is likewise a significant contribution to commemorating the 50th anniversary of the assassination of Grigoris Lambrakis, and the establishment of the Lambrakis Democratic Youth movement.

We have collaborated closely with Panos Trigazis in recent decades, both on the National Council to collect the German reparations owed since the end of World War Two, and in the effort to achieve common action and collaboration among the forces of the Left. We have collaborated in other international activities, such as the protests in Genoa and the solidarity missions to occupied Palestine.

Our common friendship with Michalis Peristerakis also brought us together in many activities, though Michalis passed away in 2011 and did not live to commemorate the 50th anniversary of the first Marathon Peace March with us.

The message in Panos Trigazis' book is the need for constant vigilance and struggle in the cause of peace, which is fragile in our region, especially at the crucial geopolitical crossroads of the Eastern Mediterranean and the Middle East, as shown by the tragic carnage in Syria.

* * *

From the Dove's Beak
Nikiforos Vrettakos

The great Greek poet and campaigner for peace and democracy, Nikiforos Vrettakos, who for two years contributed a column to Roads of Peace *under the rubric 'From the dove's beak', wrote movingly about Grigoris Lambrakis for the magazine's memorial issue in June 1963.*

There are strong proofs confirming that the nation exists. The life and death of Grigoris Lambrakis was one such proof. A glorious proof to confirm that this nation – which suffered conquest and occupation, and was then taken over by its own saprophytes – has kept its noble roots intact. That it exists and resists and that, deep inside, it is full of vital juices, ready to nurture the trunks of eternal trees. That inside it there is an independent life, an independent destiny, and an independent sun.

That it is studded with Marathon fighters who defend the very ideal of Athens from the barbarians' spirit. The trouble is that these Marathon fighters have been robbed of their armour and all means of defence, and deprived of their freedom, the bright prerequisite of existence for Marathon fighters. Despite which, they exist. Lambrakis' life and death have proved their existence.

Lambrakis became a consolation to us, restoring our hope and the spirit of virtue; he became the breeze of a beautiful Greek May, stirring the leaves of our soul – the leaves of the nation – this fine and selfless man, who is now dead and deserves to be adorned with the most exquisite blossoms we can gather, and to be bedecked with flowers by all generations who will come to this land of ours.

Starting as a young man, he never ceased fighting for the good. He entered the field and never left it. Very early in life he discovered that this field has many directions; it doesn't end anywhere, but continues even in death; and that a man's strength does not run out – it is enough to claim the championship of many sacred events up to the end of his life. That, to his very last breath, he would use this strength to win a race; to make it a smile of faith in the leering faces of his executioners.

On this field he met people who needed support; he met the destitute whom he treated free of charge; he met his homeland being ridiculed and dragged wounded through the streets; he saw people fighting and the country being laid to waste; he saw disaster coming toward us in giant strides. And, as he was fast, he ran everywhere on the eternal human field. He did not need approval or applause. The applause he heard within him was sufficient.

And finally he saw the goal of his greatest feat, which cannot be achieved by one or two or three, but needs the participation of all peoples on earth who, all together, will also be in danger of losing it unless they take up the lighted torches of his predecessors, with long strides, great courage, a great soul and a great heart. He saw the goal of peace. Peace for all. Peace for Greece, peace for the world. Peace for man, animals and plants. All of life united in brotherhood to confront an immediate threat, greater than which no other exists. Onward!

He ascended the Mound at Marathon, and covered his chest with the inscription *Hellas*. Yes, from the top of this tumulus and from Greece, this country of the sun, where 'April and love dance and laugh', where more than anywhere else one can discern that this world is too beautiful to be handed over to the devouring flames without a fight, he had to set out on a Marathon run for mankind, which continues to this day.

Lambrakis – magnificent, unbending, godlike – walked down the steps of the Mound at Marathon and started out. He got as far as Thessaloniki, where he fell. From there he continues. Onward!

Bravo Lambrakis!
Run Lambrakis!
Victory is ours!

* * *

A True Angel of Peace
Leonidas Kyrkos

Grigoris Lambrakis' action for peace was closely associated with the local organisations of the Greek movement. This is the text written by Leonidas Kyrkos[1] in 2003 for M. Arvaniti-Sotiropoulou's book Password: Lambrakis.

I first heard of Grigoris Lambrakis through his athletic successes. He was already an idol among young people. Tall, well-built, he claimed one record after the other in the long jump and triple jump and was crowned champion in both these events in the 1935 Balkan games in Istanbul.

I got to know him personally in the first of the great peace marches from Aldermaston to London early in April 1963. We were part of the group of marchers from Greece, representing the Greek Committee for International Détente and Peace (EEDYE), which had been established on the initiative of EDA (United Democratic Left) in 1955. Its president then was Andreas Zakkas, former minister of labour in the Plastiras government. Chronologically, the first secretary was L. Kyrkos. On the Aldermaston March, Manolis Glezos and Spyros Linardatos were with us. Grigoris took part in the march with all his heart. He was enthusiastic and tireless! He would get lost in the multi-coloured crowds, running from the head of the march to the end, writing his impressions in his journal, and spending time with the Buddhist monks who, throughout the march, kept beating their drums and chanting their prayers.

Grigoris Lambrakis was elected Deputy for Piraeus in 1961, in collaboration with EDA. In 1962, he was elected vice-president of EEDYE together with Michalis Kyrkos, Periklis Argyropoulos, and Nikos Kitsikis. The manager of the office at 21 Patission Street was Leonidas Nasiakos and special secretary was Nikos Theodoropoulos.

In Athens, an active group with Angelos Diamantopoulos, Nikos and Anna Solomos, Markos Dragoumis, Angelos and Anna Fokas, Gioula Linardatou and others inspired people in local districts, in the world of art and culture, and ordinary people with an uplifting atmosphere and inexhaustible initiatives. These people, together with many others, organised the activities of EEDYE, spreading its anti-war message against the bases of death, and favouring peaceful co-existence. In post-Civil

Nikos Nikiforidis

War Greece the desire for peace was intense, and peace committees sprang up everywhere and raised the flag bearing the symbol of the world peace movement.

Grigoris was always animated and energetic; a true angel of peace, he ran everywhere, spoke impassioned words, motivated, organised and activated.

From its first steps, the peace movement became a target for the parastate, which pursued it relentlessly. The word 'peace' was equivalent to betrayal for those in power. In 1951, Nikos Nikiforidis was executed in Thessaloniki because he was gathering signatures under the Stockholm Appeal against nuclear weapons. He was the first martyr to the cause of peace.

At a rally in Piraeus in 1958, at which Zakkas and others spoke, the 'dissidents' made their appearance for the first time. Security police and thugs of all types gathered outside the Municipal Theatre, prevented people from entering, and threw rocks and broken chairs at the dauntless peace-lovers, despite which the rally took place. President Zakkas left with a few bruises. It was a foretaste of the events in Thessaloniki where Lambrakis would be assassinated.

A landmark in the peace movement was the first Marathon march, organised by Greece's newly constituted Bertrand Russell Youth League for Peace and Disarmament, and EEDYE. Disregarding the ban on the march, and after breaking through the endless police cordon, Grigoris raised the flag bearing the peace symbol over the ancient mound and then, like a contemporary Marathon runner, carried it to Athens together with a small group of marchers for peace, the first of whom was Gioula Linardatou.

The peace movement was now indomitable, but the forces of intolerance and violence organised their counter-attack. In Thessaloniki the 'dissidents' – the parastate under orders from General Mitsou of the Gendarmerie – attacked Lambrakis on 22 May 1963. Mortally injured, he battled with death for days. It was his last fight, which the people watched with bated breath. Then they inundated Athens to attend his historic funeral.

With his struggles and sacrifice, Grigoris Lambrakis sparked a huge movement, particularly among young people, led by the Lambrakis Democratic Youth. The champion on the track and in the struggle for peace became an eternal symbol of the victory of humankind over savagery and the forces of war.

Footnote

1. Leonidas Kyrkos (1924-2011) was a Greek national resistance fighter and leading left-wing politician who was elected many times as Deputy and once as MEP. He spent five years in prison under the junta of the colonels, and held the posts of president and general secretary of the Communist Party of Greece (Interior). Together with Charilaos Florakis, leader of the Communist Party of Greece, he founded the Coalition of the Left and Progress (Synaspismos), and eventually joined the Party of the Democratic Left.

Preface

In 2013, we commemorated the 50th anniversary of the assassination in Thessaloniki of Grigoris Lambrakis, Deputy of the Left, assistant professor at the University of Athens Medical School, and leading figure in the Greek peace movement. In the same year we celebrated the 50th anniversary of the first Marathon Peace March, which was a landmark in the growth of the peace movement during the difficult years after World War Two and the Civil War in Greece.

Many events were organised to mark these anniversaries; one of which, dedicated to Michalis Peristerakis, was held at the Municipality of Athens Cultural Centre, with guest speaker Tony Simpson, Co-ordinator of the Bertrand Russell Peace Foundation and editor of *The Spokesman* journal. These events were part of a programme of action entitled *Year of Lambrakis*, which was supported by SYRIZA, the Coalition of the Left and the official opposition party in Greece. SYRIZA proposed that the Parliament of the Hellenes honour Grigoris Lambrakis, which it did early in June 2013.

This book was written as a contribution to the *Year of Lambrakis*. It is the product of many months' – if not years' – work. Above all, it is the product of the author's rich experience during more than 40 years' active participation in the Greek and international peace movements, which he joined after the dictatorship in Greece, having already acquired significant experience as a student in London and as an anti-dictatorship activist in Greece between 1970 and 1974. The book is introduced by the legendary Greek Resistance fighter and historical leader of the Greek Left, Manolis Glezos, who is today a SYRIZA member of the Greek Parliament. Dr. Maria Arvaniti-Sotiropoulou, President of the Greek branch of International Physicians for the Prevention of Nuclear War, has also made an important contribution to the book's creation.

The Greek Left, and more generally the democratic movement in Greece, has formed strong links with the Labour Movement in Britain and its political expressions over many decades. Bertrand Russell himself identified with the anti-fascist, democratic and peace-loving struggles of the Greek people and took an active part in the campaigns to release thousands of political prisoners after the Civil War ended in 1949. And when the Bertrand Russell Youth League for Nuclear Disarmament was established in Greece early in 1963, the relations between the movements in Britain and Greece became much closer and more productive. These relations were the antithesis of the Greek people's painful experience of official British policies, especially the military intervention of December 1944 that paved the way for the devastating Civil War in Greece (1947-1949).

The tradition of British solidarity with Greece dates from the Greek War of Independence of 1821, for which British support was very strong, and was represented above all by Byron, but also by Shelley, Keats, Bentham and many others. Again it is the British trade unions and leading figures of the British Left, such as Tony Benn, who have been the prime movers, by taking part in the Greece Solidarity Campaign. Until the end of his life, Ken Coates was in the front ranks of this movement. The Bertrand Russell Peace Foundation continues the noble tradition to this day.

Useful information for this book has been drawn from many sources, including the account by Peggy Duff entitled 'CND and Greece' (from her book *Left, Left, Left*, published in 1971), and Michael Randle's statement to Panos Trigazis about relations between the anti-nuclear movements in Britain and Greece.

This book was originally published in Greek in April 2013 by Taxideftis of Athens. It was translated by Judy Giannakopoulou.

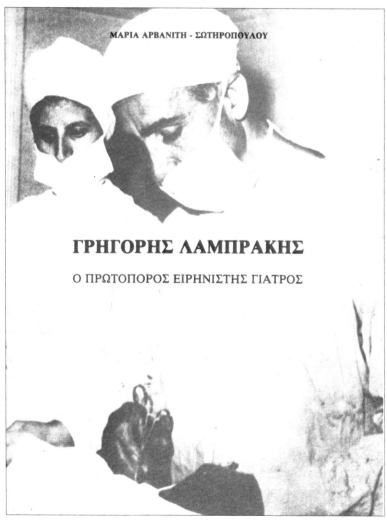

Lambrakis the medic

Introduction

Panos Trigazis

My encounter with Lambrakis

When Grigoris Lambrakis, Member of Parliament for the United Democratic Left (EDA), was murdered in 1963, I was a pupil at the Boys' High School in Pirgos, a town in Ileia, on the coast of the Peloponnese. On May 23, the day after he was attacked, my older brother Giorgis and I were walking to school as usual through the rural district of Katarachio. Along the way we passed many of the town's kiosks, where I was in the habit of sneaking a look at the sports news in the local and Athenian newspapers. That day, my attention was drawn by the assassination of Lambrakis in Thessaloniki (described as 'attempted' until he died on May 27), reported on the front pages under banner headlines. Some of them had also reprinted the historic photograph of Lambrakis walking from Marathon, arms stretched out, holding the black banner from the Aldermaston march, with the word ΕΛΛΑΣ on one side and *Greece* on the other.

I remember being impressed by one headline that said: 'Tonight I'm going to kill somebody'; a phrase uttered by Gotzamanis to the carpenter and furniture maker Giorgos Sotirhopoulos a key witness in the later trial.

'Look what this says!' I shouted to my brother, who was signalling me to keep my mouth shut because there was a police station nearby.

That was my first encounter with Lambrakis.

In November of the same year, the fall of the right-wing government (ERE) under Konstantinos Karamanlis precipitated parliamentary elections, in which our mother's brother, Aristotelis (Telis) Georgoulias, was an EDA candidate for the Prefecture of Ileia. He had fought in the Resistance, and had been exiled and imprisoned for his left-wing views. Our parents Agisilaos and Astero were poor farmers raising ten children and dreamed of educating them all, so they worked day and night and never became involved in politics. For us children, however, our Uncle Telis was something of a family legend, whose exploits we had been hearing about for years. The story of his part in the great escape of 27 communist political prisoners from Vourla prison on 17 July 1955 was like a fairytale to us.

Giorgis – who had always been rather a daring child, and hung out with children of left-leaning families in Pirgos, especially with our cousin Yannis Zoupinas – suggested that we go to the big EDA campaign rally in the main Pirgos square (today Sakis Karagiorgas Square), where the lawyer Pausanias Kanellopoulos, who headed the EDA ballot in the prefecture, was scheduled to speak. Uncle Telis was standing on the platform with the other candidates, and as soon as Giorgis saw him, he left my side and rushed over to the platform to hug him. My brother's bold act (at least that was how it struck me then) scared me. I was afraid of malicious comments and the whispering that it might have generated in our little community, which could have harmed our family, given the conditions of anti-communist terrorism prevailing then. But the atmosphere changed, as did my mental state, when a large group of young people flocked into the square carrying banners bearing the phrase 'LAMBRAKIS LIVES'. They were members of the Lambrakis Democratic Youth (LDY). The letter Z, which represents the Greek word *zei*, meaning *he lives*, became a rallying cry among young people. Later, I went to Athens where I met my cousins Giorgis and Tasoula Georgoulias, who were both active members of LDY.

Late in 1969, at the age 20, I left for England. There I was profoundly influenced by the Costa-Gavras film *Z* – based on the book of the same name by Vassilis Vassilikos, with Yves Montand playing the part of Lambrakis, and music by Mikis Theodorakis – which I saw at the Curzon Cinema in central London early in 1970. The film was a major event for the Greeks in London, especially for exiles and people opposed to the junta, who carried on intense discussions in the coffee shops of Bayswater (*Il Barino* was the name of our usual haunt) about

*1964. Telis Georgoulias with his family and comrades at the
2nd Marathon Peace March in 1964*

how the assassination of Lambrakis was an omen prefiguring the imposition of the military-fascist junta in Greece on 21 April 1967.

In London I met Tony Ambatielos and his wife Betty, and joined the Communist Youth of Greece in 1970; the anti-dictatorship struggle brought me into contact with the British peace movement, the Anti-Colonial League, headed by the Socialist Lord (Fenner) Brockway, and other movements. As a member of the Co-ordinating Committee of Overseas Students Organisations (CCOSO) in Britain, I met people from all over the world. That was when I first came in contact with the slogan 'One Race, the Human Race' and embraced wholeheartedly the idea of international solidarity.

After receiving a postgraduate degree, I returned to Greece in late 1979 to do my compulsory military service. I had started working in the tourism sector when the leadership of the Communist Party of Greece (KKE) honoured me by proposing that I do my party work in the peace committee. Thus, in June 1981, I was elected General Secretary of the Greek Committee for International Détente and Peace (EEDYE), of which Grigoris Lambrakis had been vice-president from

Betty and Tony Ambatielos

1962 until he was assassinated in May 1963. In this position, where I remained until 1991 (when I was elected to the Political Bureau of the Central Committee of the KKE, and replaced at EEDYE by Giorgos Harissis), I worked with significant campaigners for peace in Greece and abroad; many became friends with whom I collaborate to this day.

I identified with many of the movement's ideas and initiatives. From the post of General Secretary of EEDYE, I worked closely with major figures in the arts and letters, such as the poet Yannis Ritsos; composers Mikis Theodorakis and Manos Loizos; actors Manos Katrakis, Aleka Katseli and Lykourgos Kallergis; engraver Tassos; author Dido Sotiriou, and many others. I contributed to organising the Peace Route from Olympia to New York, which saw the flame of peace carried from the cradle of the Olympic idea to the United Nations headquarters, where the Second Special Session on Disarmament was due to begin in June 1982.

In carrying out my duties as EEDYE secretary I apprenticed alongside KKE MP and MEP Vassilis Ephraimidis, Prof. Alkis Argyriadis, President of the Athens Bar Association, Evangelos Mahairas and Dinos Tsiros. I frequently travelled abroad, contributed to events in honour of Nikiforidis and Lambrakis, took an active part in organising large-scale marches from Marathon to Athens – but also from Kerasitsa to Tripoli – and worked to promote the common actions of the Greek peace movement with those of other countries. Our communication with other peace movements was assisted by an English-language EEDYE *Bulletin* produced by Judy Giannakopoulou.

I became associated with the Palestinian movement and, in particular, with the Palestinian Liberation Organisation (PLO). In 1984, I was among those involved in establishing the International Olympic Centre for Peace and Culture (DOKEP), based in historic Olympia, with an enthusiastic collaborator in the person of Spyros Foteinos, then Mayor of Olympia. That was when we drafted the Appeal for a Modern Truce during the Olympic Games, an idea that was later adopted officially by the Greek state and the UN in the form of The Olympic Truce. One of the great memories from that period was the visit to Athens of the legendary long-distance runner Emil Zátopek, nicknamed the 'Czech Locomotive', who warmly supported our initiative.

Those were difficult years in Greek-Turkish relations – the Peace Committee was on trial in Turkey, as was its president and honorary ambassador, Mahmut Dikerdem, but the solidarity and collaboration between the movements of our two countries nevertheless developed. In Greece there was the Committee for Greek-Turkish Friendship, with Mikis Theodorakis as president and members Stephanos Linaios, Giorgos Papapetros, Makis Trikoukis, Alekos Mytakakis and Wing Commander (ret'd) Giorgos Pattas, with whom I worked closely.

In short, working for peace was for me a great political and ideological school that played a significant part in my decision to support the effort for renewal by

With Charilaos Florakis, KKE leader, at Dikeli, Turkey

'perestroika' in the then Soviet Union, and the new political thinking in international relations that we represented.

From my time in the peace movement I have retained the spirit of collaboration that I acquired through the constant effort to build unity of action and to expand the movement; to enrich the forms of action; to foster originality and inventiveness; to produce new ideas and to promote alternative proposals. For example, at one of the EEDYE congresses, the goal had been to draw up and propose our own 'draft agreement for a denuclearised Balkans'. In the 1980s, we drew many ideas from the emerging anti-nuclear movement in Europe; encircling military bases such as the camps at Greenham Common in Britain, at Comiso in Italy, and so on. The mass mobilisations and interventions of the anti-nuclear movement made it the third, unofficial negotiator in critical summit meetings between the US and the USSR about détente and disarmament. That was when the phrase 'diplomacy of the peoples' came into being.

In Greek-Turkish relations we tried to encourage the diplomacy of the peoples by organising a joint Mytilene-Dikeli Peace Festival in 1990, which provided the opportunity for Charilaos Florakis – then president of the Coalition of the Left and Progress, whom I accompanied – to meet Haydar Kutlu and Nihat Sargin, the leaders of the United Communist Party of Turkey. On the initiative of the peace movements EEDYE and AKE (Independent Peace Movement), a Greek-Turkish conference had been held on 21-22 April 1989 at the Journalists' Union of the Athens Daily Newspapers (EΣHEA), on the subject of a mutual reduction in military spending by Greece and Turkey; other than at this event, the festival meeting was the first time this issue had been raised.

European Network for Peace and Human Rights

In the post-Cold War period I continued my participation in the international peace movement in close collaboration with the Bertrand Russell Peace Foundation and its President, Ken Coates, whose initiative it was to convene a conference of peace movements at the European Parliament (31 January – 1 February 2002), which led to the establishment of the European Network for Peace and Human Rights, of which I continue to be a member.

* * *

My interest in Lambrakis and in publicising his contribution has never diminished, even after the Cold War ended, with the concomitant decline of the peace movements. In 1998, on the occasion of the 35th anniversary of Grigoris Lambrakis's assassination, I invited fellow campaigners and comrades to join in sending the following proposal to the Speaker of the Parliament, Apostolos Kaklamanis:

> Mr Speaker,
> Grigoris Lambrakis, who we are commemorating today on the 35th anniversary of his assassination by the fascist parastate, is one of the great figures in the history of twentieth-century Greece.
> The story of Grigoris Lambrakis is unique. Through his struggles, he honoured the high office of Deputy of Parliament as few others have done. He brought glory to Greece as an athlete. He fought for its freedom in the ranks of the National Resistance. He contributed a great deal to the science of medicine as a university teacher and practitioner. He promoted national reconciliation during an extremely difficult period. He became a nationwide and international symbol through his struggles and sacrifice in the cause of peace.
> In the conviction that we have a special bond with the story of Lambrakis through our participation in the peace movement, the undersigned have taken the initiative of proposing to the Parliament of the Hellenes that it honour the Marathon runner for peace.
> We believe that this honour will send a strong message to the young generation who are searching for human-centred dreams and values; it will constitute a strong condemnation of the fascism and racism that are reappearing dangerously in Europe and in Greece, and a confirmation of our people's resolve to contribute to the cause of peace, at a time when it is being sorely tried in our region, and when our national issues are at a critical turning point. Grigoris Lambrakis must take his rightful place beside Rigas Velestinlis as a herald of inter-Balkan collaboration.

The letter was signed by Tassia Andreadaki, Georgios Dolianitis, Manolis Glezos, Nikos Kaisaris, Lykourgos Kallergis, Stephanos Linaios, Nikos Markatos, Michalis Peristerakis, Lakis Santas, Sotiris Siokos, Maria Sotiropoulou and Panos

Trigazis, representing the full spectrum of post-dictatorship peace organisations.

The right to peace, the right to life

Alkis Argyriadis

The struggle for peace has been an essential part of progressive and liberation movements throughout history. The dawn of the nuclear age, after the holocausts of Hiroshima and Nagasaki, changed the very concept of war – a nuclear war could mean the end of life on our planet. For the first time in history, the human race faced the threat of total self-destruction; the struggle for peace and nuclear disarmament has now become, quite literally, a fight for life.

The events of the Cold War period, together with the organisation of people's struggles for peace all over the world, triggered initiatives to establish the right to peace as a fundamental human right. This issue preoccupied the United Nations General Assembly, which adopted the Declaration of the Right to Peace (12.11.1984). In Greece, the distinguished attorney Alkis Argyriadis, president of EEDYE, in an article he wrote for its magazine *Roads of Peace (Dromoi tis Eirinis)*, recommended that the right to peace be instituted as he had proposed at a UNESCO conference in Malta. In addition, at EEDYE's 11th Congress in 1991, he discussed the adoption of a 'Charter for the Right to Peace' in order to encourage discussion of the issue among the Greek people, but also that it be claimed by the Greek state.

The text of the EEDYE proposal, which I helped draft, is as follows.

At this time, the guarantee of the right to peace means:
1. To recognise human life as the supreme value, and the right of all nations and all people to decide their own fate and to enjoy the fruits of their labour.
2. To promote peaceful co-existence as a universal precept in international relations and renunciation by all of the use or threat of force.
3. To reject the doctrines of 'nuclear deterrent' and 'balance of terror'.
4. To ban the production, possession and use of nuclear, chemical and other weapons of mass destruction.
5. To democratise international relations, to serve human beings, their development, their rights and freedoms.
6. To reduce military spending drastically and to transfer these resources to growth, to environmental protection, to eliminating hunger and illiteracy, and to combatting unemployment, disease and the scourge of narcotics.

For Greece in particular, the proposal was formulated:
1. We regard our national independence and sovereignty as non-negotiable and irreconcilable with the presence of foreign military bases on our soil.

2. We propose that the prohibition of nuclear weapons on our soil, and of visits to our ports by warships that are either nuclear-powered or carrying nuclear weapons, be enshrined in the Constitution.

3. We believe that military procurements and the activities of the war industry must be subject to parliamentary and social control.

4. Training and information must serve peace and humanitarian solidarity, and be opposed to violence and racism.

5. The peace movement must be supported by the Greek state in order to achieve its goals.

I believe that this proposal retains its full significance to this day. The issue came up again many years later when Manolis Glezos, Maria Arvaniti-Sotiropoulou and I sent a report to the Greek Ombudsman (25.9.2009) on the occasion of parliamentary elections, pointing out the Greek state's violations of the 'right to peace'. The report stated:

We invoke the Universal Declaration of Human Rights (article 3), the Declaration of the Peoples' Right to Peace of the UN General Assembly (12.11.1984), and the Declaration of the Human Right to Peace (1997) by the General Secretary of UNESCO Federico Major, in which it is noted that 'peace is a prerequisite for the exercise of all human rights and obligations'.

Based on the above and on the realisation that war leads to the abolition of all rights, but also that peace is not just the absence of war, we believe that the right to peace is being violated in the following instances:

1. Greek citizens are paying a very high price for expensive armaments (550 euros per capita per year); global military expenditure amounts to 202 dollars per capita (data from 2007). In addition, these expenditures are being made with no transparency and in the absence of multi-party parliamentary control.

2. Our country is a participant in the war in Afghanistan, which has already lasted for eight years and has had many civilian casualties. This war now costs 50 billion dollars a year, an amount representing 50% of international aid to all poor countries.

3. Only a very small number of asylum-seekers in Greece, most of whom are war refugees, enjoy the right to asylum. In 2008 the percentage of applicants granted asylum was 0.05%: just 14 were granted asylum out of a total of 29,573 applications examined at the initial level, according to the UN High Commissioner for Refugees.

4. Last January, when Israel's war was raging in Gaza, it was discovered through the US Pentagon that the Greek port of Astakos was used to move US weapons to Israel. This involvement became more serious after the recent publication of the Report of the UN Special Research Committee documenting the war crimes committed during these hostilities.

5. Xenophobia and racism are spreading throughout Greece and Europe, cultivated by specific forces that exploit insecurity and the acute problems created by the financial crisis. These phenomena are directly contrary to a culture of peace and co-existence and 'may endanger the friendly relations between peoples, the collaboration between countries and international peace and security', as noted by the Declaration of the UN World Conference against Racism (Durban, 2001).

We are aware that the legal basis for this appeal is weak. But it is time for initiatives to be taken, as has already happened in other countries, to recognise the right to peace as a human right, directly interwoven with the right to life.

The process of amending our country's Constitution is expected to begin this year; a proposal could be submitted that would guarantee the Constitutional right to peace.

* * *

Fifty years have passed since Lambrakis was assassinated, during which major events and developments have taken place in Greece and in the world at large. The most dramatic of these, in my view, was the dissolution of the USSR in 1991, which dealt a heavy blow to the global balance of power and signalled the end of the hopeful attempt at perestroika. These developments could not even have been imagined in 1963.

I would have hoped, after the great battles fought over many decades, and particularly after the end of the Cold War, that we would now be able to say 'the peace movement is no longer needed'. Unfortunately, however, the peace movement is needed today more than ever before, and could become even more important. It could constitute a deterrent to the arrogance of the mighty of the earth, whose choices threaten humankind with the dissolution of international law and any international guarantees of security and peace that were won in the 20th century and were the crowning achievements of the anti-fascist victory in World War Two, starting with the establishment of the United Nations in 1945.

Lambrakis the athlete

CHAPTER 1

The Leap from Kerasitsa through Sport to Science

Lambrakis' Life and Diaries

'I write down the most important events of my life, ones that recently affected me and my character, directly or indirectly; a gift to my old age, a remembrance.'

Thus began Grigoris Lambrakis' diary, on 27 December 1936, when he was already a medical student and Balkan champion. It is tragic that such valuable material would not be used for reminiscences in his old age, which never came, but for the careful study of his youth, which he was unable to bring to light himself.

Grigoris Lambrakis was born in Kerasitsa in the prefecture of Arcadia on 3 April 1912. Land-locked Arcadia was cut off from progress and saw its villages gradually abandoned as their inhabitants migrated to the cities. Lambrakis lived through the seemingly endless wars suffered by the Greek people, from the Balkan Wars to World War Two and the Civil War in Greece.

Lambrakis' family, with many children and little money, provided him with the first opportunity to exercise his natural abilities – endurance, perseverence, sensitivity and humanism. He experienced social injustice at first hand, along with the growing belief in a better future to be achieved through courageous and persistent struggle. His father, Georgios Lambrakis, had a total of 14 children from two marriages. The majority were girls – 'bills to be paid' according to the custom of the period, which dictated that for a girl to be marriageable, she had to be accompanied by a substantial dowry, as women did not work outside the home at that time. One of Georgios' sons was obliged to migrate to the United States. In this rural community, their father was a man of many trades: farmer, carpenter and shopkeeper.

Grigoris attended elementary and secondary school locally, always excelling. As he wrote in his diary:

> In September 1919, I registered at the elementary school in my village ... In September 1924, after passing some exams, I registered at the Greek School (middle school) in Tegea near Tripoli. After three years' study, I received my certificate in 1927 ... In September 1927, I registered, after passing exams, at the 1st Gymnasion (secondary school) in Tripoli. Five years later, I received my secondary school leaving certificate.

In 1931, after secondary school, Grigoris attended the Panagiotopoulou Commercial and Bookkeeping School in Piraeus, in accordance with his father's wishes that he assist at home and in the family shop. His older half-brother, Thodoros, was already a doctor in Piraeus. Thodoros supported and helped those who dared to break away and were forever lost to the fields and houses of village life.

Grigoris initially disciplined himself to the family programme. He finished school and tried in vain to work up some enthusiasm for his father's dreams. 'My father is pleased because he'll have an educated man as his successor in business,' he wrote. But such a life could not satisfy one born for greatness.

'No decision had crystallised in my mind,' he wrote in his diary. 'I finished Commercial School in June 1932. One day in early July, I left for the village, happy to think that I'd be able to keep the books for the shop ... I arrived in the village amid joy and commotion ... How enthusiastic I was ... Unconsciously, however, I observed that my enthusiasm was unintentionally evaporating ... My thoughts now turned to Piraeus ... My father saw me looking downcast; he could see that I was a child unlike the others, and this weighed on his spirit. He was braiding garlic outside the door of the shed, looking towards the church. It was a summer's morning in 1932 when, after a lot of thought and with great emotion and pain, my father said to me:

'My boy, I don't want you to be a farmer all your life ...'

And that was it. That was the spark that lit the torch of my passion to go forward and surmount the many hurdles I later encountered in order to study. I thank my father for saying this. If he hadn't done so, I would never have dared tell him I wanted to be a doctor or even that I wanted to leave the village and life on the land. Then I wondered what would become of the house if I left, and my spirits suffered too, but I very much wanted to be a doctor. I wanted everything: to be at home and in Piraeus as well ...

'All that's fine ...' my poor father kept telling me. 'I know what you want to do and I support your decision. But what's going to happen at home later, when I die? What will happen to the houses, to all those fields I bought with so much honest sweat? Besides, learning this job (medicine) will take six years and you'll need 50,000 drachmas a year. I've got girls and can't afford it! Thodoros can't help. What can we do?"

Fortunately, Thodoros, like a *deus ex machina*, provided the solution, by undertaking to finance Grigoris' studies. Their mother's relief was palpable after the problem was solved. 'Blessings on you, my child,' she said, 'may God enlighten you and may you become a good man and escape from this tyranny.' His father continued to waver. 'He was semi-pleased,' Grigoris wrote, 'he was uncertain':

'Get on with it, my boy. See that you become a good man. The girls and I, as long as I can, will look after the fields, and God will provide.' Most of the time, that was what he said. But there were a few sharp moments when he spoke with the yellow face of a bitter father:

'With such wealth, Grigoris, prospective grooms will descend in hordes to party...'

* * *

This is a moving description of the atmosphere prevailing in a province that was fighting tooth and nail to keep its children at home; meanwhile, the capital city, Athens, was also striving, but to send the bold away. Free education then was not even a dream, and as declared many years later by the university faculty, medicine was intended only for the wealthy. What poor young man could afford to spend so much studying for so many years and then, for as many years afterwards, to acquire his specialism, after which he would be in unsalaried employment for a while? And how could any hard-working student dare try and obtain a degree from a school where you passed examinations only after showing the receipt for the textbook written by the professor?

So, students such as Lambrakis were rare and exceptional. 'Being the son of a father with many children, and having excellent marks as stipulated, I was able to register free of charge for three consecutive years,' he wrote, with justifiable pride. His admission to university coincided with Thodoros' problems. In the newspaper *Simaia* of 12 July 1934, we learn that, owing to political disagreements, the Tzaneio Hospital in Piraeus fired Svolopoulos and Thodoros Lambrakis, who were serving as director and department head respectively. Thus these two doctors came to establish the White Cross clinic in the city of Piraeus, which became a refuge for its residents during the difficult years of Nazi Occupation, and where Grigoris was present from his student years, always beside Thodoros. His student years during the Metaxas dictatorship were distinguished by athletic success. He appears to have divided his energies between study and the track.

Champion of Greece and the Balkans

Athletics provided another great landmark in the career of Grigoris Lambrakis.

'At the same time as my training at Medical School, I devoted myself, and still do, to classical athletics, to the 100-metre and 200-metre race, the long jump and the triple jump,' he wrote in an autobiographical note in 1939. 'I have been champion of Greece since 1935, and between 1935 and 1939 I was also Balkan champion, with ten firsts in the Balkan games and a new Balkan record.'

After Grigoris' assassination, the *Roads of Peace* columnist, who wrote under the pen name Athletikos, described the great athlete Lambrakis in a moving article in the special issue of June 1963:

'... Among thousands of mourners, a group of familiar names of his ordinary fellow athletes stood out, a little dot in the multitudes. Together with the pain in their grieving hearts, they were holding the trophies of the champion – shiny silver postscripts to a life dedicated forever to endeavour, performance and success: Ragazos, Thanos, Eleutheriadis, Arvanitis, Domnitsa Lanitou, Karagiorgos, Mavroeidis, Marinakis, Petrakis, Skouris, Sphikas and others, Balkan champions and others of the past and present, his fellow athletes and successors who followed the funeral procession with tears in their eyes … As they passed under the columns of the Temple of Olympian Zeus, which the last rays of sunlight had bathed in melancholy light, the former fellow athletes and the current Balkan champions turned their gaze towards Ardettos hill, as a last farewell to the lamp of the great athlete whose immortality was assured …

In the funereal silence, trophies and damp eyes spoke of triumphs and successes, bringing back to life an unforgettable era in our athletic history:

1934: A young athlete appears in the gymnasium of the Piraeus Syndesmos. His trainer, Takis Sakellariou, predicted a brilliant future on the track for this youth from Kerasitsa.

1935: A new name is written in the lists of Greek champions: Grigoris Lambrakis, 19 years old, first nationwide in the triple jump with a record of 13.62m. In the same year, on 31 August, he broke the panhellenic record in the long jump with 7.15m (the previous record was 7.02m, held by Kyprios Papamichail). With this jump Lambrakis was catapulted into the firmament of Greek sports as a star of the first magnitude. A week later, in Istanbul, he won his first Balkan victories, with 7.10m in the long jump and 14.13m in the triple jump!

1936: Once again on the podium as Balkan winner: he came first in the triple jump in the Balkan games in Athens, with a leap of 14.19m.

1937: Among the Balkan winners in Bucharest, he is again crowned winner in the long jump, with 7.05m.

1938: Another jewel in the crown of Balkan successes: first in the long jump with 6.94m.

1939: It is rare that an athlete experiences such acclaim. In the Balkan games that year, he ascended to the top of the podium as Balkan winner no fewer than four times: first in the long jump with 7.35m; first in the triple jump with 14.19m; first in the 100 metres with 11 seconds; first in the 200 metres with 22 seconds!'

Grigoris Lambrakis was, quite literally, a super athlete – during his six years in active sport he won 12 Balkan victories and the title of Greek champion ten times; he also took part in the Berlin Olympic Games, in 1936, and the World Student Games, in 1937, in Paris.

The best year in Lambrakis' sporting career was 1938. In August that year, he broke three national records in the long jump. In the Greek-Egyptian games he increased his distance to 7.16m. In the regional games he jumped 7.20m, and in the Pre-Balkans he shattered this record with a leap of 7.37m, a record that remained unbroken for 21 years. In autumn 1959, in the Balkan Games in Bucharest, a young athlete named Dimos Maglaras from Katerini triumphed with an unbelievable jump of 7.51m, taking over the torch from Lambrakis.

The columnist Athletikos described the meeting between the now practising obstetrician Grigoris Lambrakis with his successor in the long jump:

'It was a quiet afternoon in the autumn of 1959, at his old clinic near the Museum, when the now mature Lambrakis had an unexpected visitor, a shy young man with an unbuttoned shirt and startled eyes, who was trying to find the right words with which to tell the doctor why he had come.

"My name is Maglaras…"

There was great emotion on both sides. Words were unnecessary. Wearing his white coat, the doctor grasped the young man's hand, then hugged him like a son. Congratulations were a formality. Afterwards they spoke in the language of the heart and of the most noble human feelings. This diffident youth came, bashfully, to announce the end of an era. And the mature man accepted the announcement of his own end, with as much joy as this young man who was experiencing his own beginning.

"I've been waiting 21 whole years for this moment," said Lambrakis emotionally, "And it came just as I was starting to be disappointed at not seeing a young athlete come to take over from where I left off so long ago. I thank you and congratulate you. There is, however, one thing I want to tell you from my own experience on the track: being an athlete is difficult and requires total dedication. But the most difficult moment is that of success. The success that suddenly raises you up high can also destroy you as a human being if you have not prepared yourself for it. You need a strong psychological underpinning to keep yourself up there and to be able to go even higher, which is your duty as a proper athlete."

Maglaras listened with his head bent, modest, enigmatic. He neither disclaimed nor promised anything; he could only thank Lambrakis. Two or three days later, he was invited back to the clinic on Patission Street. The doctor had invited him to give him a cup that he had ordered especially for his successor – for the youth who smashed his long-standing record to smithereens.'

Lambrakis ended his career in competitive sport in 1940. His diary gives the date as Tuesday 2 April 1940 at 5:30 pm, and the place as the old Olympic Stadium, but he continued to serve sport in other capacities. During the German occupation, his most important activity was through the Association of Greek Athletes (EEA), which he helped establish in 1943 and served as its vice-president, with Renos Frangoudis as President, Giorgos Thanos as General Secretary and G. Karagiorgos as Treasurer

According to Thanos, this association played an historic role throughout the occupation. It maintained the continuity of sport in Greece, and without EEA, without Lambrakis, there would have been a gaping hole in the history of athletics in Greece. Lambrakis played a very significant role in EEA by organising a system to monitor athletes' health and provide care. He then transferred this organisation to SEGAS (Hellenic Amateur Athletic Association) in the early years after the occupation, when he became a member of its board. Unable to maintain it, he set up another body, the Health and Care Fund for Athletes (TYPA), and continued his work as its president.

For Lambrakis, sport was not an end in itself. He saw it as a vehicle for global brotherhood. In 1961 he said:

'Let's spend less money on war and more on sport. Besides, Greeks, Turks, Bulgarians, Romanians, Yugoslavs and Albanians have today forgotten what they once knew in the trenches with guns in their hands. Today they're competing over who will run fastest or throw the discus furthest. Tomorrow this friendship will be consolidated.'

In October 1960, long before friendship committees were established between Greece and Turkey, Lambrakis said prophetically:

'… Regarding the close friendships created by athletic events, I can tell you this: I was good friends with Tefik, the Turkish triple jump athlete, who is today a senior naval officer. He used to say we'll always be friends, even though our fathers were bitter enemies.'

True to the Hippocratic Oath

'I graduated from university, started my specialism at the Marika Eliadi Maternity Hospital in Athens, where I did my internship, and in 1941 I shared a room with Stamos Houlis, next door to the Averoff Prison, at Lombardou 129. I lived in this room throughout the German occupation until March 1945.'

In 1988, the Panhellenic Medical Society against nuclear and biochemical weapons published a book entitled Grigoris Lambrakis: The Pioneering, Peace-Loving Doctor, *an exceptional work by Dr. Maria Arvaniti-Sotiropoulou which focused on Lambrakis' social and scientific work. With the author's permission, some excerpts and information from this book follow.*

Lambrakis practised medicine according to the Hippocratic model in times of peace and war. In May 1939, he received his MD with the designation *Magna cum laude.* In the same year he was appointed – initially without salary – to the Marika Eliadi Maternity Hospital (also known as 'Helena's' because it was financed by Eleftherios Venizelos' wife Helena, a close friend of Marika Eliadi). In 1940, he joined the armed forces and served in the Reserve Officers Academy on Syros, where a commemorative album has been preserved in which he wrote:

'Ten days before leaving the school as a doctor to go to the front, I thought of asking my fellow students to write a few words in this notebook for me to remember them by, if I survive. As their leader at the school, I tried to convey to the students the notion of love and solidarity … Dedicated to my dear fellow students who, I hope, will be alive and well at the end of this cruel war (21.12.1940).'

Then Lambrakis joined the resistance organisation EAM, early in 1943. Thodoros was already with the resistance in the mountains, in free Greece, where he organised medical care for resistance fighters. By March 1943, Grigoris was living at the White Cross clinic and, on 7 August 1945, was appointed lecturer at the Tzaneio Hospital. That same summer, the Germans captured their other brother, Mitsos, who had been betrayed and was to face the firing squad. His farewell letter to Grigoris has been preserved, in which he wrote:

'My dear brother Grigoris,
I know that my execution will bring you great sorrow, but want you to know that I am not being shot for theft or dishonour. I have always worked honestly. So please console

all our family. Vengeance against the informers. My only complaint is that I have not enjoyed life fully and am dying before my time. I kiss you. Goodbye forever.'

Fortunately, Mitsos was not executed, but later he was sent to a concentration camp in Germany where he managed to survive, even though he was severely handicapped.

Grigoris did not lose heart. No contribution seemed adequate to him, given the needs of the times. In Athens he was in the front ranks of protests and demonstrations, while at the same time continuing his social and humanitarian work. The White Cross clinic was placed entirely at the disposal of the soup kitchens to help the Greek people survive the genocide by starvation imposed by the Nazis. Thanks to Lambrakis, health care and follow-ups were organised for athletes and no small number of lives were saved by his efforts.

During the Civil War, true to his Hippocratic oath, Lambrakis worked day and night at the Marika Eliadi Hospital looking after the wounded, although sick with jaundice himself. Upon retreat of the Democratic Army, he found himself accused of 'anti-national action' and was jailed in Goudi.

In August 1949, he opened his own clinic in Athens (50 Patission Street). Here, every Wednesday, he treated destitute patients free of charge, while continuing to visit Tripoli once a month where, at the clinic of his uncle K. Tsoukopoulos, he examined his compatriots without charge. Also, as his fellow sportsmen testified, Lambrakis would never take money from athletes.

In this field as well, Lambrakis was a leader. It was typical that at his first question time as a Deputy or Member of the Hellenic Parliament, the first question he asked was about supporting agrarian clinics. Because, even then, he could see that a properly organised health care system would have to start by

ΕΚΑΣΤΗΝ ΤΕΤΑΡΤΗΝ 5-7 Μ.Μ

Ο Κ. ΛΑΜΠΡΑΚΗΣ

ΔΕΧΕΤΑΙ ΤΟΥΣ ΑΠΟΡΟΥΣ

ΔΩΡΕΑΝ

'Every Wednesday between 5-7 pm
Dr. Lambrkis sees poor patients free of charge'

ΓΡΗΓΟΡΙΟΥ Γ. ΛΑΜΠΡΑΚΗ
ΥΦΗΓΗΤΟΥ ΤΗΣ ΜΑΙΕΥΤΙΚΗΣ & ΓΥΝΑΙΚΟΛΟΓΙΑΣ ΕΝ ΤΗ ΙΑΤΡΙΚΗ ΣΧΟΛΗ ΤΟΥ ΠΑΝΕΠΙΣΤΗΜΙΟΥ ΑΘΗΝΩΝ

ΓΕΝΙΚΗ
ΕΝΔΟΚΡΙΝΟΛΟΓΙΑ

ΦΥΣΙΟΛΟΓΙΑ ΚΑΙ ΠΑΘΟΛΟΓΙΑ ΤΩΝ ΕΝΔΟΚΡΙΝΩΝ ΑΔΕΝΩΝ

ΜΕΤΑ ΠΡΟΛΟΓΟΥ **ΓΕΩΡΓΙΟΥ ΙΩΑΚΕΙΜΟΓΛΟΥ** ΑΚΑΔΗΜΑΪΚΟΥ,
ΤΑΚΤΙΚΟΥ ΚΑΘΗΓΗΤΟΥ ΤΗΣ ΠΕΙΡΑΜΑΤΙΚΗΣ ΦΑΡΜΑΚΟΛΟΓΙΑΣ
ΕΝ ΤΩ ΠΑΝΕΠΙΣΤΗΜΙΩ ΑΘΗΝΩΝ, ΔΙΕΥΘΥΝΤΟΥ ΤΟΥ ΒΙΟΧΗ-
ΜΙΚΟΥ ΕΡΓΑΣΤΗΡΙΟΥ ΤΟΥ ΘΕΡΑΠΕΥΤΗΡΙΟΥ "Ο ΕΥΑΓΓΕΛΙΣΜΟΣ».

ΤΟΜΟΣ ΠΡΩΤΟΣ
ΥΠΟΦΥΣΙΣ - ΥΠΟΘΑΛΑΜΟΣ - ΘΥΡΕΟΕΙΔΗΣ

ΑΘΗΝΑΙ 1954

*Lambrakis' text book on
general endocrinology*

supporting the people in the provinces, and that the only way to do this was to motivate doctors to go there, and not, as was later implemented (initially by the junta, but continues to this day), with police measures sending inexperienced fresh graduate doctors to 'care for' unfortunate farmers.

Tireless researcher

Lambrakis was a tireless researcher. More than 40 papers are cited in his biography. His research was initially conducted in the biochemistry laboratory at Evangelismos Hospital under G. Ioakeimoglou; later, at the Pathology-Anatomy Lab under I. Katsaras; at the General Chemical State Laboratory; at the Greek Pasteur Institute; at Marika Eliadi, and at the Public Maternity Clinic.

Thirty of his scientific papers were collected, as was the reprint of his participation in discussions at the Athens Medical Association and the Obstetrical and Gynaecological Society. Nineteen of these papers have been preserved in summary form in a booklet published in 1949 entitled: *Gr. Lambrakis: Career and Scientific Papers.* This booklet, which also served as a curriculum vitae in his application for an assistant professorship, contained his own presentation of his career as a scientist. He likewise noted his membership in the Obstetrical and Gynaecological Society of Athens, Athens Medical Society, the Surgical and Medical Society of Athens, and the Association of Evangelismos Hospital Scientific Staff. Lambrakis' diary describes his path to this candidacy:

'In 1945 I decided to apply for an assistant professorship. In February 1949, I went to Varybombi (for peace and quiet), sat in the Karadima hotel where I worked day and night on the CV to accompany this application. When I returned to Athens, I went straight to the typographer Pelekanos and started printing it. I submitted it on 30th March 1949.

2 December 1949.
Louros was appointed by the Faculty to propose my candidacy for the assistant professorship.'

During the same period, he was asked to appear at the Transit Centre in Patras. He continues in his diary:

'24 April 1950.
Louros submitted his proposal for my candidacy. I am in Patras studying for my orals

at the Faculty. I studied on my way to Patras on the train and bus. I studied in the Majestic Hotel there, and night and day I'm still studying in my clinic at 50 Patission St.

12 May 1950, Friday 7 pm
I was called to the School for the oral examinations. Thodoros came with me. I am fully aware of the seriousness of the moment. Having started in the countryside wearing a little village cap, I'm now knocking on the door of the Faculty of Medicine asking to be elected assistant professor. Thodoros gives me courage.
7:30 pm
First K. is called in. Then 40 minutes later, he comes out frowning because he says Professor M. assailed him and he's afraid they're going to reject him.
7:50 pm
"Lambrakis!" they shout. I go inside calmly, and find myself facing some thirty professors who scrutinise me. Inside, in absolute silence, the Dean gets up and says to me:
"Mr. Candidate, please outline to us briefly the subject of your paper in application for the assistant professorship."
I started talking calmly, discussing my experiments clearly and succinctly. By the eighth minute, I had won them all over. By the tenth minute, I was finished. I felt I'd won. I'd won the race.
The Dean got up:
"Does anyone wish to submit a question to the candidate?"
Then Mr Sk. got up and told me about a typographical error in my book! Nobody else asked anything.
"The Candidate is free to leave," said the Dean.
I went out full of joy. Thodoros kissed me. He had heard everything because he had asked Thymios the clerk to let him into the antechamber of the School auditorium.

18 May 1950
I've been going back and forth to Patras. I am in the meantime studying for the orals in front of an audience.

23 May 1950, Wednesday.
I went to the university to find out when I was to speak. They decided on Friday. Louros gave me the topics. I took them and went straight to my clinic. I took with me as many books as I thought I'd need, and went by taxi to Thodoros' clinic in Piraeus. Thodoros wasn't there. I slept for a while to pull myself together and at 5 pm I opened the books and started studying. I chose the subject of 'sterility' and studied day and night. By Thursday evening, I was ready for the lecture in the amphitheatre the next day.

26 May 1950, Friday, 6:15 pm
We're outside the amphitheatre. At 7:10, P.P was called in. I wait outside. My name is called. I go inside and walk up the stairs to the podium, taking deep breaths so that my voice is calm. At the beginning I can hear my voice cracking. After a few moments, I calm down. I look steadily at the same point. When I finished the clinical part and got into the biological aspect of the diagnosis of sterility, I realised that I'd won this race, too. The audience was listening very carefully to what I said. I was absolute

master of myself. The professors were nodding their heads favourably. I finished and went out.

I waited nervously for the decision, pacing back and forth in the courtyard with Thodoros and P. Suddenly I see a hand reaching towards me and a voice saying;
"Mr Lambrakis, my congratulations. You have been elected."
I am an assistant professor. That night I slept at Thodoros' house.
"What I am, I owe to you," I told him. "I know how much this has cost you and how much you have suffered for me. I am very grateful.'"

CHAPTER 2

The Peace Movement

'Resolved, courageous human beings, with head high and a strong inner sense of self-preservation and social responsibility can generate an unprecedented, invincible chain reaction of peace among their friends, in their unions, neighbourhoods and villages throughout the country.'

From a Greek Peace Committee brochure entitled
Save Greece – Save Humanity, May 1957

I
The roots of the modern peace movement[1]
The Perpetual Peace of Immanuel Kant

The idea of world peace is interwoven with the intellectual awakening of Europe during the Enlightenment in the 17th and 18th centuries. The primary example is the teaching of the German philosopher Immanuel Kant, for whom 'perpetual peace' was not a chimera or an idea bereft of content, but an obligation deriving from the very nature of Reason as the attribute that elevates human nature above that of other animals, and should always take precedence over his instinct to dominate, which leads to war. Kant admits that a peaceful atmosphere between people living in a community is not the 'natural state', which is that of war;[2] thus, Kant calls upon man to transcend his own natural inclination to violence and to elevate himself through the power of Reason. This ideal of eternal peace is incompatible with that of global governance, but expresses the need for countries to reach an agreement on the laws that will facilitate the peaceful settlement of their differences without undermining their sovereign rights.

According to Kant, to achieve the coveted perpetual peace, man's will must prevail over his instincts, and policy must be harmonised with ethics. The main foundation for the ethics of peace which Kant envisioned was a 'federated union' of states that would function in accordance with six normative principles.[3] First, no peace treaty can be held valid when it has been made with the secret reservation of the material for a future war. Second, no independent state shall be acquirable by another state through inheritance, exchange, purchase or donation; it is no commodity, rather a community of people which cannot be conceived as anyone's asset or property. Third, standing armies shall be entirely abolished in the course of time – as Kant says, spending on armaments ultimately makes peace less tolerable than war. Fourth, no national debts shall be contracted in connection with the State's external disputes; for Kant, the support offered by economically sound states to weaker ones creates dependence that can lead to bankruptcy and war.[4] Fifth, no state shall forcefully interfere with the constitution or government of another state.[5]

Sixth, no state at war with another shall use such modes of hostility as would render mutual confidence impossible in future peace-time, such as assassins or poisoners, violation of a capitulation, the instigation of treason, and such like.[6]

Kant envisioned international law with reciprocal concessions that would lead to an ever-expanding state of nations and would ultimately include all peoples on earth.[7] In his essay on *Perpetual Peace*, he lays the foundation for a cosmopolitan, multicultural society – a society of the world's citizens – one that could be described as internationalist. The essay was written in 1795, when Europe was convulsed first by the events of the French Revolution and then by the rise of Napoleon. It was the product of the philosophical, revolutionary and political currents that led to the first great awakening of the peoples of Europe. Kant's ideas can certainly be rebutted, and indeed there are counter-arguments in terms of both their essence and how realistically achievable they are. Particularly in the light of international law, the question of how achievable or utopian Kant's views are continues to be an object of reflection and dialogue between politicians, analysts and philosophers to this day.[8] The fact remains, however, that the approach to ethics in political life, as expressed through the teleological nature of perpetual peace, whether utopian or not, has changed political thought and is today an on-going experiment in international relations. The demand for peace remains universal,[9] and even though perpetual peace may be utopian, this does not mean that we, as rational beings, should behave as though it were not possible.[10]

Victor Hugo, the visionary

Hugo envisioned a Europe of brotherhood, freedom and, above all, peace. He was a friend of Greece, but also a supporter of every oppressed nation fighting for freedom, from Cuba and Mexico to Belgium, Italy and Ireland. In Hugo's view, there were no great or small nations; they all had the same value and the same right to freedom and peace. Hugo's life spanned the 19th century, an era characterised by revolution and the awakening of the peoples through the burgeoning of science and technology, the industrial revolution and the development of ideologies that have influenced people's lives profoundly from that time on.

In the middle of the 19th century, various sages, intellectuals, politicians, authors and poets established the International League of Peace and Freedom to disseminate its ideas in Europe. Victor Hugo was among the League's members. In 1869, the League held a conference in Berne, Switzerland, to which Hugo, who was unable to attend, addressed a letter that has become extremely relevant today, about the problem of peaceful democratic and socialist brotherhood between the peoples of Europe. Some excerpts summarising Hugo's thoughts on European and world peace are set out below:

'Fellow citizens of the United States of Europe! From now on, you are justified in proclaiming that war is evil, that this glorified murder, arrogant and regal, is dishonourable, that human blood is precious, that life is sacred. Civilisation tends to unite (...) and merge nations into Humanity, which is the Supreme Unit. (...) Who do borders serve? They serve leaders, who divide the peoples in order to rule. Borders require guardhouses and every guardhouse needs a soldier. 'Prohibited' is a word belonging to every authority, every censor, every tyranny. Every human disaster is generated by these borders, this guardhouse and this soldier.

The king (...) needs the soldier. (...) Kings need armies, and armies need war. Otherwise there is no reason for their existence. It is very curious that man consents to murder another man without knowing why. The art of despots is to divide people into armies. (...) It is certain that wars are fought on various pretexts but there was never a more important cause than the army. By removing the army, you also remove war. But how to abolish the army? By getting rid of the despots! Kings agree on one point, on the perpetuation of wars. You think they're quarrelling? Not at all. They are helping each other.

(...) So, let us walk unanimously towards our goal, which I once designated as replacing the soldier with the citizen. On the day this revolution takes place, the day when people will throw out men of war, their worst enemies, these people will once again find their unity and love. Civilisation will be called harmony, and it will bring with it creative work and the light of the Soul, Peace.'

It is hard to imagine an explanation of the concept of the Peace of the Peoples that is more eloquent, or richer in political significance.

International peace law
From The Hague to San Francisco

Towards the end of the 19th century, the idea of peace had already begun to take on a legal dimension. In 1899, the first International Peace Conference was held in The Hague to work out ways to resolve crises peacefully, to prevent wars and to codify regulations for the conduct of war. The first Hague Convention, consisting of four main sections and three added statements, was signed on 29 July 1899 and entered into force on 4 September 1900. Briefly, it provides for the peaceful settlement of international disputes and prohibits the use of certain types of modern military technology, such as aerial projectiles and explosives, poison gas, and bullets that change shape in the human body. It also established a permanent arbitration court.

A second peace conference was held to supplement the initial Hague Convention, amending some parts and adding others. The second Hague Convention was signed on 8 October 1907 and entered into force on 26 January 1910. It provides, among other things, for the peaceful resolution of international disputes, for limiting the use of force, and sets out the rights and obligations of neutral powers, as well as conventions regarding war at sea.

Following the violation of the Convention terms in World War One and after the dreadful carnage in the trenches, the League of Nations – predecessor of the United Nations – was established in 1919 by the Treaty of Versailles to 'promote international co-operation and to achieve peace and security'. The League of

Nations had noble goals, but failed abysmally in its mission, resulting in the devastatingly criminal tragedy of World War Two.

In 1945, representatives of 50 countries met in San Francisco at the United Nations Conference on International Organization with the purpose of drawing up the United Nations Charter. Between August and October 1944 at Dumbarton Oaks in the US, the delegates had negotiated proposals drafted by the representatives of China, the Soviet Union, the United Kingdom and the United States. The Charter was signed on 26 June 1945 by representatives of the countries present. The name 'United Nations' was devised by US President Franklin D. Roosevelt and used for the first time in the United Nations Declaration on 1 January 1942 when, during World War Two, representatives of 26 nations committed their governments to continuing the common battle against the Axis forces.

The United Nations was officially established on 24 October 1945, when its Charter was ratified by China, France, the Soviet Union, the United Kingdom and the United States and the majority of the other signatory states. Its fundamental purpose, from the moment of its founding to this day, has been to protect and preserve peace, and to prohibit war as a means of resolving international differences. The human race emerged from World War Two – the most devastating war in human history, which cost the lives of more than 50 million people and incalculable material damage – and resolved to uphold the slogan 'no more fascism – no more war'. The tragedy of Hiroshima and Nagasaki launched the nuclear age in 1945, aroused the global conscience, and rendered urgent the need to organise the struggle for peace and disarmament on a global scale.

II
The first globalised movement

> I am terrified by the idea that one day some secret
> may be found that will shorten the road to the obliteration
> of individuals, peoples and entire nations.
>
> *Charles Montesquieu*
> *Lettres persanes*, 1721

'To hate war, go to Auschwitz,' Greek author Elli Alexiou once said. The same can also be said of Hiroshima, which I visited in August 1991 and, of course, Nagasaki. It's only when you're in Hiroshima, visiting the Peace Park, standing in front of the monument to the victims and listening to the *Hibakusha* (survivors) that you understand why the slogan 'No More Hiroshimas' stands alongside 'Never Again' of World War Two, and why it has been such an enormous force in awakening and mobilising people from one end of the earth to the other. That was when the peace movement became globalised.

The picture with the hands of the clock stopped at 8:15 contains the devastating memory of when time stopped – when Hiroshima was reduced to ashes by 'Little

Boy', the first atomic bomb, dropped by the US military on this beautiful Japanese city. On 6 August 1945, at 8:15 am precisely, an entirely new era began; for the first time in history, the human race had acquired the ability to wipe itself off the face of the earth. Greek author Antonis Samarakis made a good point when, speaking at a peace demonstration in Delphi in 1986, he said that 6 August 1945 was the first day of 'Year 1 AH' (after Hiroshima).

'The war was won but not the peace,' wrote Albert Einstein to a friend just after World War Two ended. 'People were promised that they would be free of fear but, in fact, fear has increased greatly since the end of the war.'[11]

After World War Two came the Cold War and the nuclear arms race. Eric Hobsbawm observed in his book *The Age of Extremes* that World War Two had scarcely ended when humanity was plunged into a third world war, a very special sort of war.

Einstein was one of the first to raise his voice in protest against the new threat to humankind. In 1946, together with eight US nuclear scientists, he established the Emergency Committee of Atomic Scientists, of which he was president, undertaking to inform the American people about the dangers inherent in nuclear weapons. He wrote in an article in 1947 that the military attitude of that era was even more dangerous than the one that had prevailed earlier, because offensive weapons had become so much more destructive than defensive weapons; this attitude would inevitably lead to a pre-emptive war and to the abolition of citizens' rights.[12]

Frédéric Joliot-Curie

Until his last breath in 1955, this great scientist never stopped warning, protesting, and corresponding with national leaders to foster the growth of the international peace movement. In his joint manifesto with Bertrand Russell (the Russell-Einstein Manifesto), which he signed just before he died, Einstein supported the establishment of a world peace movement of scientists, which became known as the Pugwash Movement, after the village in the Canadian province of Nova Scotia where its founding conference was held in 1957.

Meanwhile, major steps had been taken towards organising the peace movement on a global level. On 6 August 1948, the third anniversary of the bombing of Hiroshima, the first World Congress of Intellectuals for Peace met on the ruins of the Polish town of Wrocław, which had been destroyed by the Nazis. The participants included Frédéric and Irène Joliot-Curie, Pablo Picasso, Pablo Neruda, Paul Éluard, Jorge Amado, Nazim Hikmet and Eugénie Cotton; there were also

Petros Kokkalis

Elli Alexiou

Greeks – the surgeon Petros Kokkalis and author Elli Alexiou. The latter subsequently wrote, 'Wrocław was then just a memory. When we arrived, we saw a devastated town. An endless expanse of debris and piles of ruins, over which hung the curse of war.'

This was followed, on 20 April 1949, by the World Conference of Peace Forces, held simultaneously in Paris and Prague as the Cold War did not permit all the delegates to gather in one place. This conference decided to set up a World Peace Council, which was established a year later in Warsaw, with headquarters in Vienna. Its first President was the French scientist Frédéric Joliot-Curie, who had been awarded the Nobel Prize for Chemistry jointly with his wife Irène, daughter of Marie and Pierre Curie.

The first worldwide nuclear disarmament campaign was organised by the World Peace Council (WPC) by decision of its conference in Stockholm on 15 March 1950, when signatures were gathered under the Stockholm Appeal, which read:

WE DEMAND the outlawing of atomic weapons as instruments of intimidation and mass murder. We demand strict international control to enforce this measure.
WE BELIEVE that any government which uses atomic weapons against another country will be committing a crime against humanity and should be dealt with as a war criminal.
WE CALL ON all men and women of good will throughout the world to sign this appeal.

More than 500 million signatures from citizens all over the world were collected under this appeal. But supporters of the old doctrine of 'if you want peace, prepare for war' or 'mutually assured destruction' (MAD) were not pleased with these developments. They targeted Frédéric Joliot-Curie, President of the WPC, who in reply to the US delegate to the United Nations said, in 1952:

'You accuse me of prostituting science, because I have risen up against the criminal use of the discoveries of the great Pasteur and because I appeal to public opinion to prevent the continued development of microbiological warfare. For me, those who prostitute science are those who ushered in the atomic age by annihilating 200,000 citizens in Hiroshima and Nagasaki.'

In 1955, the global movement for nuclear disarmament received a huge boost from the publication of the famous Russell-Einstein Manifesto in which these two renowned scholars called upon mankind to think about the nuclear age in a new way; to rid themselves of the doctrine of nuclear deterrence, of nuclear weapons, and of the disastrous view that a nuclear war could be won. 'Remember your humanity and forget the rest' was one of the key phrases in the manifesto.

III
The Greek Peace Movement is born
Nikos Nikiforidis – first martyr of the anti-nuclear movement

'We want to find the way. To obstruct the pathway to war. To involve young people in the struggle for peace. To build schools. To plough the wasteland. To build smokestacks. To do away with corruption. So that life is a song not a groan.'

Nikos Papaperiklis (Glafkos) Avgi, 31.8.1952

After the War and the Civil War, the demand for peace was multidimensional in Greece. It was rooted in international developments, in the grim reality of the Cold War and the threat of nuclear weapons, but also reflected the profound inner need of the Greeks to heal their many wounds. By 1 January 1950, 2,289 partisans had been condemned to death, 16,783 to life imprisonment, 5,485 were awaiting trial, and 15,000 were exiled.

It is fitting that the emblem of the United Democratic Left (EDA), founded on 3 August 1951, contained the three words *Peace, Democracy* and *Amnesty*; likewise, that the name chosen for the newspaper of the United Democratic Youth of Greece (EDNE), created on 15 August 1951 with the merger of left-wing youth organisations, was *Guardians of Peace*.

EDNE was in the front ranks of the growing peace movement. 'It promotes the most noble ideals of peace and democracy, civil liberties and independence among young people,' wrote its secretary, Potis Paraskevopoulos, on 7.8.1953 in the newspaper of the Left, *Avgi*.

On 18 January 1951, 14 members of the Democratic Youth Peace Front were arrested; one of them was its main organiser, Nikos Nikiforidis.

The promulgation of the Stockholm Appeal was the first mass peace mobilisation in post-war Greece, which had emerged from the Civil War in ruins, bloodied and deeply divided. Gathering signatures under the Appeal (a form of struggle which many underestimate today) involved major risks at that time. This is immediately obvious from the fact that the young peace activist, Nikos Nikiforidis, was arrested, tried, and sentenced to death by an extraordinary court martial and executed on 5 March 1951 in Thessaloniki. As Spyros Kouzinopoulos wrote with heavy irony in his book *The Execution of Peace: The Nikiforidis Case*:

'In Nikiforidis's file, which has been preserved in Yedikule, the ... terrible charge, always written in black pencil, on which he was tried, convicted and executed was "Attempt to promulgate subversive ideas".'

Emphasised in parentheses was the vital evidence: Stockholm Appeal for Peace.

Nikos Nikiforidis was executed at the age of 22. He had finished secondary school by taking night courses because he worked in the morning. He was an excellent student who wanted to continue his studies but was exiled to the island of Ikaria at the age of 18. After Ikaria, he was again sent into exile, this time to the island of Makronisos, where he was badly tortured and then released in the spring of 1950, without having signed the so-called declaration of repentence, but with serious health problems due to post-traumatic stress.

Manolis Badourakis, a fellow exile of Nikiforidis, said that Nikos had been tortured frequently on Makronisos. His main torturer was the notorious lieutenant Dimitris Ioannidis, who 'reformed' thousands of Greeks on that barren, hated island during the dictatorship of the colonels (1967-74), together with other members of the junta who undertook to 'save' Greece and doomed Cyprus.

After returning from exile, Nikiforidis became secretary of EPON in the Athens district of Pagrati, but soon left and went to Thessaloniki, where he began to take an active part in organising the peace front. He was arrested on New Year's Eve 1951 and imprisoned in the fortress of Eptapyrgio (Yedikule). He was remanded to trial, sentenced to death and executed in the Seich-Sou forest, the usual site of executions.

Nikos Nikiforidis's last words before he died were: 'Long live peace! Long live freedom for all humanity!'

Founding the Greek Peace Committee (EEDYE)

In spite of terrible problems, the Greek peace movement was undaunted. It opposed Greece's membership in the Cold War organisation of NATO in 1952, the agreement between the US and Greece (12.10.1953) to build US military bases on Greek soil, and the unchecked use of our land, air and sea space by US and NATO forces.

The time had come for a nationwide peace organisation. On 15 May 1955, a proclamation was published that had been signed by 77 public figures.[13] Below is an excerpt from the text:

> 'As a result of our continued shared anxiety, we the undersigned address this appeal to all those who are aware of the monstrous threat that hangs over us, and we ask them to rally together with peace-loving people all over the world, in a strong joint effort capable of persuading those who govern the large states, that it is their duty to hasten and satisfy – according to the true spirit of the Founding Charter of the United Nations – the most earnest and humanitarian desires of all peoples: the significant limitation of conventional weaponry, the abolition of all weapons and other means of mass destruction, the rejection of war as a means of resolving international disputes and the restoration of sincere and stable relations of friendship and mutual respect between all countries, because it is only in this way that Peace, the supreme good, will be secured for every Nation.'

This was followed by the founding of the Greek Committee for International Détente and Peace (EEDYE), which was accompanied by the creation of many local peace committees. At the same time, EEDYE developed international contacts as testified by the messages it received on its first birthday on 15 May 1956 from Frédéric Joliot-Curie, President of the World Peace Council; Nikolai

Tikhonov, President of the Soviet Peace Committee; Gordon Schaffer, President of the British Committee; Emmanuel d'Astier, Vice-President of the French Movement, and others.

Between 5-9 April of the same year, the Greek movement was represented at a World Peace Council meeting held in Stockholm. Despite the fact that the sole item on the agenda was disarmament, we read in a text from the period that the Greek delegation[14] raised the issue of Cyprus, which the other delegates received warmly. Nikos Kitsikis noted in his speech that, for Greece, disarmament was literally a matter of life and death, pointing out that 53% of the state budget was devoted to military spending, which also absorbed about 85% of the three billion dollars in American aid that Greece had received since 1947.

The strengthening bonds between the Greek and international movements were confirmed by the award of the WPC Peace Prize to author Nikos Kazantzakis in 1956.

A significant increase of peace activities is noted in an EEDYE brochure published in 1957 and entitled *Events against missile-launching bases in Greece*. In it, among other things, we find a list of the public figures who supported these events, including many intellectuals and artists.[15]

The movement continued to grow in the following year as well, when the Greek Committee for Balkan Understanding was founded, with Stamatis Mercouris, former Mayor of Athens and father of Melina Mercouri, as its President. On 9 May 1958, the first issue of the magazine *Roads of Peace* was published, initially in the format of a small four-page newsletter.

The year 1958 was marked by the first counter-demonstrations against the peace committee similar to those organised five years later in Thessaloniki that provided the setting for the murder of Lambrakis. This initial event took place during an open meeting of EEDYE in the Municipal Theatre of Piraeus on 12 January 1958. The President of the Piraeus Branch was then G. Tzatzanis. Chairing the meeting with him were MP Tasos Voulodimos, three former government ministers, Andreas Zakkas, Leon Makkas and Periklis Argyropoulos, retired Admiral Gianikostas, retired Rear Admiral Antonopoulos and three mayors.

Outside the hall, the counter demonstration had been organised by the so-called Association of Repatriates from behind the Iron Curtain. Many 'dissidents' were scattered around in the boxes and in the hall; for 2½ hours they shouted abuse ('murderers', 'crooks', etc.) and insulted the speakers and friends of peace in an effort to break up the meeting. When the first hour passed and they had not achieved their goal, they became even more aggressive, to the point of throwing chairs onto the stage.

As Yannis Voultepsis reported in his book *The Lambrakis Case*, nobody was arrested and nobody was sued for what had happened that day in Piraeus. All the hecklers remained anonymous. The right-wing newspapers presented them as 'repatriates from Tashkent' and as having been 'prisoners of gangs', but many were recognised by the citizens present as neither of these.

The movement's progress could not be stopped. In 1960, the Labour Movement for Disarmament and Peace was established and its headquarters, like that of EEDYE, were at 21 Patission Street.[16]

Roads of Peace

Giannis Theodorakis

'We were going to meet in Syntagma Square and I was nervous, because after many years, I was on my way to meet the man I knew as Petros, whom I hadn't seen since the occupation. I always thought the legend surrounding him had to do with some gun he'd used to shoot invaders in the streets of Athens. But I was shortly to realise that the weapons which had made him so famous were his smile and the thousands of ideas generated by his mind in a second. Petros was his code name; Dimitris his real one. It was Mimis Despotidis.

"Do you write?" he asked me.

"Not very well, I'm afraid."

"You'll write, and you'll be a good journalist."

I had no right to refuse. Mimis had just got out of prison.'

This story was told by poet and journalist Giannis Theodorakis[17] at an event in 1988 to commemorate the 30th anniversary of the first issue of *Roads of Peace*.

'Journalism fascinated me, as it does all young people, but in 1960, when I was already 28 years old, I believed that I had definitively chosen the path of the cinema. But, one hot summer afternoon that year, my life changed forever. Without giving it too much thought, I followed the roads of peace.'

Nikiforos Vrettakos

The growth of the peace movement was reflected in *Roads of Peace* which, from a four-page small-format newsletter had, by 1960, grown into a magazine with a variety of material. The magazine initially had 36 pages but increased to 40 in 1961 and again to 56 in 1962. The publisher of the magazine was Andreas Zakkas and its director Leon Koukoulas, then President of the Society of Greek Authors; the first chief editor was Markos Dragoumis and, after 1963, it was Manolis Papoutsakis. 'From the dove's beak' was the name of the regular current events column written by the poet Nikiforos Vrettakos, who was succeeded, in January

1964, by the Cypriot author Theodosis Pieridis. 'The Midas notebook' was the name of the regular commentary column which became 'The Croesus notebook' in March 1964, reflecting the change of writer. The inimitable cartoonist Bost (Mentis Bostantzoglou) satirised developments in his own way. A regular column by physician Nikos Zakopoulos (who likewise became known as an author) gave medical advice; other noteworthy columns were 'Leda and friends', with advice for women and, of course, the sports column, edited by *Athletikos* (*The Sportsman*).[18]

The case of Giorgos Maniatis is worth noting. At the age of 19 he went to Belgium as a worker where he was recruited into the Foreign Legion and sent to fight in Algeria. Once there, his sympathies shifted to the Algerians, which invited personal repercussions. He then began to contribute to the magazine, writing a series of articles entitled 'How I escaped from the Foreign Legion'.

The working atmosphere at *Roads of Peace* was described by Giannis Theodorakis:

'Without further discussion, I went in the afternoon to Ippocratous Street. There, in the offices of EEDYE, the staff were waiting for me: Markos Dragoumis, Lena Dragoumi, Sophia Koukouvitou, Kostas Koukouvitis, Andreas Rambavilas, Alekos Skaldalis. And Mimis...

We started enthusiastically, with confidence in each other. Against us we had the entire state, as well as the parastate.[19] We also had the innate obstacles present in our movement; prejudice, fear of responsibility, distrust ... But Mimis was able to deal with them. *Roads of Peace* was something totally new, at least in the publishing history of the Left.

The problem we had to confront was how to make a bi-monthly information bulletin into a monthly broad-circulation magazine. Contributors had already been found. The names of some were so strictly protected that I never found out who they were. Except for one. He revealed his identity to me during the dictatorship, when we worked together on the first edition of *Anti*. It was Mimis Papanagiotou who later became editor of *Kathimerini*. In the 1960s, his contribution to *Roads of Peace* was sports reporting ...

There was an interesting episode about the use of a full-colour cover on the magazine. Theodorakis tells the story:

'I remember the number 618. That was the number of copies of the first issue we sold. You will appreciate our disappointment when the circulation of the second and third issues was even lower. A newspaper vendor who used to give us advice on circulation told us that our magazine was the best one on the market for the Greek family, but that it needed a coloured cover depicting actors and actresses. We took his idea to heart and hastened to submit it to those responsible for the publication. They were stunned by our nerve ...

Nevertheless, the idea went forward, despite the modest black-and-white taste of the leadership. The opportunity was provided by the filming in Drapetsona of the initially banned and censored neorealist film *Synoikia to Oneiro* which showed the abject

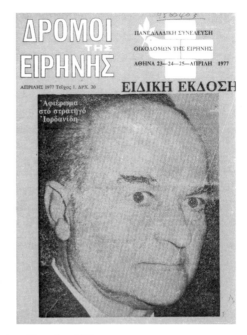

Covers of the magazine Roads of Peace

poverty of post-war Greece. It had all the sympathy of EDA, and starred popular actors Alekos Alexandrakis and Aliki Georgouli, who were featured on the magazine's first full-colour cover.

Huts, barefoot children, among whom were Aliki and Alekos … The clicks of the camera recorded the miracle. The 400 issues we sold in Attica became 4,000. In six months, our circulation exceeded 15,000!

That was how the story of our covers began. Every new face added 800-1,000 new

Vanessa Redgrave

readers. Success. And I even started to make a name for myself … Some people recognised me and said 'good work!'; others wanted to punch me.

So the colour cover prevailed, on which many known actors and other famous people were portrayed, including Aliki Vougiouklaki, Elli Lambeti, Irene Papa, Vanessa Redgrave, Brigitte Bardot, Mikis Theodorakis and Yevgeny Yevtushenko, as well as other public figures ranging from Theodoros Kolokotronis (a leading figure in the Greek War of Independence) to Bertrand Russell, Yuri Gagarin and John Kennedy. But the cover on issue 55, dated August 1962, divided our readers, because it depicted a girl wearing a bikini. Many letters were written to the editorial committee, both pro and con, but the latter appeared to prevail, so the editors had to admit in writing that the cover in question was a mistake.'

Another noteworthy episode in the life of *Roads of Peace* started in the April 1961 issue, where the terms of an international contest sponsored by the magazine *Czechoslovak Unions* were published. Contestants had to write a thousand words about disarmament, and the question put to them was: 'Suppose you were representing your country at the UN General Assembly. What speech would you make?' Thousands of people took part, among whom were 70 Greeks. One of them, a 17-year-old student named Thanassis Paparigas, received 6th prize, which was a camera.

After the dictatorship, *Roads of Peace* was re-issued by EEDYE with publisher-director Dinos Tsiros and editor-in-chief journalist Alexis Carrer. The first issue was dedicated to General Giorgos Iordanidis, first president of EEDYE after the dictatorship fell in 1974. Many people contributed articles to *Roads of Peace.*[20]

The Bertrand Russell Youth Movement for Peace and Disarmament

History has shown that young people have always been the main protagonists of all the great popular movements. Greece is no exception.

Early in 1963, the Bertrand Russell Youth Movement for Peace and Disarmament, the Greek affiliate of the British Committee of 100, was established in Athens. Its office was at 3 Asklipiou Street; its emblem was the logo of nuclear disarmament. Its first president was the independent left-wing law student, Michalis Peristerakis, and its general secretary, Nikos Kiaos. Michael Randle, peace activist and secretary of the Committee of 100 (1960-61), made the following statement about the significance of the Bertrand Russell Movement in Greece:

'The emergence of the Bertrand Russell Committee of 100 in Greece, and in particular its Marathon March of April 1963, was a great morale booster to people campaigning for nuclear disarmament in Britain. It was particularly gratifying to those of us in the Committee of 100 to see the method of non-violent direct action being used in support of a campaign for peace, civil liberty and democratic rights, especially as the influence of Bertrand Russell and the Committee of 100 was made so evident in the choice of the name for the movement.'

Bertrand Russell had established bonds with the Greek movement during the National Resistance. He recognised the sufferings inflicted on the Greek people by the British intervention in December 1944, and in the Civil War that followed, with all its repercussions. The release of Greek political prisoners after the Civil War was one of the many fields of action of this great intellectual and anti-fascist, as Giorgos Kalpadakis wrote in his essay *Bertrand Russell and Post-Civil-War Greece* (Colleagues Publishers, Athens 2012).

EEDYE's contacts with Russell started soon after it came into being in 1955. In issue 33 of *Roads of Peace*, the following message from Lord Russell to the Greek People was published:

'I would like to tell all the friends of Peace in Greece the same thing I tell friends of Peace all over the world. Nuclear war would have been a conclusive, absolute disaster. It is almost certain that nuclear weapons will sooner or later lead to nuclear war. Alliances will not protect us. War will break out in all likelihood, perhaps by accident, perhaps on the vicious initiative of one person who will be a military commander. One way or another, war is possible. The more closely you are bound in an alliance, the greater will be your suffering when war breaks out.

The entire issue of nuclear weapons is something altogether new in human history. Once you could survive a war. Today that hope no longer exists. If we do not abolish war, war will abolish us. And then we'll have a planet without life, forever and ever ...'

To return to the subject of the Bertrand Russell Youth Movement, Michalis Peristerakis wrote:

'The youth movement for nuclear disarmament was a necessity that thrived in the great reawakening among Greek young people in the early 1960s. Some of the students' demands revolved around the struggle for democracy, increased funding for education, the democratisation of higher education, protection of the right to assemble and upholding the Constitution more generally, with the abolition of extraordinary laws and measures, and the assurance of university asylum. Within this climate and under the influence of critical international developments – the nuclear threat, the Cold War confrontation, the Cuba crisis, etc. – but also the growth of the anti-nuclear movement under the dominant presence of Bertrand Russell, the Movement was what Greek young people had been seeking, outside of party labels ...'

The testimony of Andreas Lentakis[21]

The movement had an immediate impact among the young generation. One of its first activities was to propose that a peace march be held from Marathon to Athens. Andreas Lentakis, one of the protagonists in the popular movements of the period, a leading figure in the peace movement and the Left, described the events that preceded the first Marathon Peace March in a speech he made after the fall of the junta:

'The students started their struggle over Law 114 in 1962, and developed a magnificent movement. The National Students' Social Organisation (EKOF) was sweeping the schools. Late in 1962, a great movement started with the demand that 15% of the state budget be allocated to put education on its feet.

In January of 1963, 'education coaches' were travelling throughout the country and a nationwide referendum was proposed for the 15% issue, with the goal of collecting a million signatures in a month.

On 18 January 1963, secondary school teachers announced a long-term strike. Throughout the country, 7,000 teachers went on strike, an unprecedented event with 100% participation. On 23 January, elementary school teachers also went on strike, as did teachers in private education. Some 36,000 educators were on strike constantly, despite pressures and government threats. On the same day, a nationwide strike by school children was announced as a token of solidarity.'

Footnotes

1. Part I of this chapter, about the philosophical and ideological roots of the peace movement, was based extensively on a paper by attorney Yannis Gounaris, an expert in international law and General Secretary of the Citizens' Movement against Racism.
2. Kant adopted in part the Hobbesian view of the bellicose propensity of human nature, which he saw as expressing not only the wild state of nature, but also the social and political conditions where these propensities to violence are characteristic of those in power.
3. Immanuel Kant, *On Perpetual Peace.*
4. Kant's text strikes one as most apt in relation to the present situation in Greece and its dependence on the good will of its international creditors.
5. In other words, Kant rejects categorically the theory of humanitarian or peace-keeping armed interventions, and of course the contrivance of 'regime change'.
6. Here Kant lays the philosophical foundations for 'ethics in war', i.e. for international humanistic law.
7. From one standpoint, the best example of such a transnational association is the European Union. In this regard, the view should be noted of Panagiotis Kondylis who, using Kant's terminology, describes the present conditions in Europe as a 'truce' rather than as conditions that will lead to permanent peace.
8. Cf. *inter alia*, M. Dimitrakopoulos Το φιλοσοφικό κίνημα του Ευρωπαϊκού Διαφωτισμούμ *The Philosophical Movement of the European Enlightenment)*, Vol II, 2001, p. 279. Jürgen Habermas 'Global Governance' (in Greek) *Kyriakatiki Eleftherotypia & 7*, no. 181, 08/05/05, p. 24. Umberto Eco, *Kant and the Platypus*, (quoted in Greek) *Ellenika Grammata*, 1999, p. 341 and John Rawls, *The Law of Peoples* (quoted in Greek), Poiotita Editions, 2002, p. 70 & 92.
9. Kant's approach to gradual disarmament, his proposal that states be economically independent, his opposition to 'well-intentioned' peace-keeping interventions, the idea of a federated union of peoples and states and his prophetic stance on the powerful role of financial interests that can act catalytically in ensuring or seeking peace, are all impressively significant.
10. See in this regard, the Hellenic Ethics Society (http://?ethics.gr/content.php?id=20).

11. Philip Frank, *Einstein – His life and times*, (Greek edition), Kypseli eds., p. 393, Athens 1958.
12. Ibid. p. 392.
13. Among the signatories were academician Nikolaos Veis, professors Giannis Imvriotis, Haralambos Theodoridis and Kostas Tzonis; poets and authors Kostas Varnalis, Yannis Ritsos, Nikiforos Vrettakos, Dimitris Fotiadis, Tassos Leivaditis, Markos Avgeris, Agis Theros, Leon Koukoulas, Yannis Kordatos and Galateia Kazantzaki; actors Manos Katrakis, Rita Myrat, Melina Mercouri, Vassilis Diamantopoulos and Aspasia Papathanasiou; former government minister Andreas Zakkas and Deputies of Parliament Tassos Voulodimos, Kostas Dimopoulos, Xenophon Eleftheriadis, Xenophon Zanis, Nikolaos Zorbas, Dimitris Theocharidis, Leonidas Vasardanis, Christos Korakas, Emmanouil Kothris, Dimitris Papaspyrou, E. Pepas, Andreas Riziotis and Giorgos Tzatzanis.
14. Andreas Zakkas, Deputy, former government minister and Presdent of EEDYE; Nikos Kitsikis, former rector of NTUA; sociologist Dimitris Danielidis; and attorney Maria Thanopoulou.
15. These names included: A. Valakou, M. Varvoglis, D. Voutyras, N. Vrettakos, G. Gounaropoulos, A. Theodoropoulou, A. Theros, M. Katrakis, L. Koukoulas, V. Mesolonghitis, D. Bogris, Myrtiotissa, N. Pergialis, G. Sikeliotis, D. Skoura, A. Synodinou, G. Fteris, and E. Hatziargyri.
16. The first president of the Committee was Simos Hatzidimitriou and leading members were Orestes Hatzivassileiou (the next president), Vassilis Nefeloudis, Vassilis Georgakopoulos, Ioannis Lagos, Kleanthis Christodoulou, Dimitris Kolliarakis, Kostas Maragoudakis, Thanassis Tsouknidas (then Chairman of the co-ordinating committee of Working Young People), Kostas Papanikolaou, Takis Tassoulis, Antonis Tsolobos, Vagelis Tsakiris, and Vassilis Samaras.
17. Giannis Theodorakis, who died in 1996, was the brother of composer Mikis Theodorakis.
18. Journalists and regular contributors to the magazine included: Giannis Theodorakis, Giorgos Maniatis, Andreas Georgiou, Nikiforos Antonopoulos, Fontas Ladis. Contributors were S. Alexandrou, Minos Argyrakis, Dimitris Raftopoulos, Giorgos Koukas, Anna Foka, Lena Balli, Eva Patiki, Ant. Moschovakis and M. Tsakanika. The illustrations were mainly by Giannis Paraskevadis and Alekos Bouras, with cartoons by Giannis Kalaitzis and Alekos Kyritsopoulos. The magazine had correspondents in London (Panos Zemenidis and Owen Mortimer), Prague (Leonidas Theodosiadis), Sydney (Christos Mourikis) and Nicosia (Sophianos Chrysostomidis).
19. The parastate was a shadowy group of far-right-wing thugs with connections to the military and, many believed, to the palace.
20. Among the post-dictatorship contributors to *Roads of Peace* were journalists Alexis Carrer, Giorgos Tsapogas, Fontas Ladis, Lefteris Papadopoulos, Giorgis Kongalidis, Thodoris Roubanis, Dimitra Goudouna, Krikor Tsakitzian, Maria Karhilaki, Gioula Louizou, Apostolos Strongylis, Foteini Pantzia; university faculty members Savvas Agouridis, Alkis Argyriadis, Vassilis Metaxas, Thanasis Geranios, Vassilis Proimos, Emilios Koronaios, Marios Nikolinakos, Michalis Stathopoulos, Christos Frangos, Stratis Kounias, Philippos Nikolopoulos, Giannis Samaras, Maria Hourdaki and Christos Theodoropoulos; actors and artists Minos Argyrakis, Lykourgos Kallergis,

Thymios Karakatsanis, Vagelis Kazan, and Michalis Nikolinakos; authors Iakovos Kampanelis, Ermos Argaios, Manolis Gialourakis, Ioanna Karatzaferi, Pepi Daraki, Stella Karamolengou, Michalis Staphylas, Giorgos Kouloukis and Nikos Maragos; the 'generals of peace' Giorgos Koumanakos, Giorgos Pattas, Richardos Kapellos, Spyros Sermakezis and Miltiadis Papathanasiou; trade unionists Kostas Maragoudakis, Haris Papamargaris, Sotiris Siokos, Antonis Tsolompos; and peace activists Evangelos Macheras, Vagelis Hatziangelis, Kostas Kritsinis, Grigoris Petropoulos, Kostas Tsivelekas, Katerina Anthi, Giorgos Parianos, Giorgos Lambrakis, Vassilis Mantzikas, Tassos Travlos, Andreas Theofilou, Apostolos Aloniatis, Apostolos Kokolias, Giorgos Harisis, Nikos Poniros, Dimitris Aaron and others.

21. Andreas Lentakis was born in Ethiopia and studied at the University of Athens where he was a leading figure in the student movement. During the junta he was arrested, tortured and imprisoned for four years, after which he became a founding member of EDA. He was also elected Deputy with the Coalition of the Left and then, in 1993, joined Political Spring. In addition to his political life, he also wrote 23 books.

CHAPTER 3

The 1960s and the
Global Rise of the Peace Movement

I
Martin Luther King

The power of non-violence and civil disobedience

The 1960s were marked by the civil rights struggle in the United States led by the Rev. Martin Luther King, and by the great movement against the war in Vietnam. They were also distinguished by new victories of the national liberation movements, by the French May '68 and the Prague Spring of that year, as well as the first arms control agreements between the US and the USSR.

Martin Luther King was not a politican in the narrow sense of the term. He never ran for political office, which he might one day have done had he not been assassinated on 4 April 1968 in Memphis, Tennessee, at the age of 39. King was an activist, an anti-racist, a humanitarian, a champion of civil rights for African Americans, a fighter for peace and against the 'dirty' US war in Vietnam, an opponent of colonialism, and a herald of non-violence and equality.

It is particularly important that activists for peace and human rights should be

Martin Luther King

aware of what King believed and the methods he used in his struggle; this helps us to answer questions such as whether non-violence can incite people to rebel, or whether it perhaps means passivity, reduced militancy, the absence of any spirit of radical dispute, and the rejection of revolution. We also need to answer the question of whether non-violence and civil disobedience movements can bring results – whether they can be victorious.

Martin Luther King began his struggle in 1955, at the age of 26, when he was an ordinary minister in a Baptist Church in Montgomery, Alabama. It all started with the arrest of Rosa Parks, an African-American woman who refused to give up her seat on the bus to a white man. The public reaction took on the form of a mass boycott of the buses and was further aroused when King was arrested and his house torched. The movement was so broad in scale that it led to a US Supreme Court ruling that the laws requiring separate places on buses for black and white Americans were unconstitutional. It was the first victory for the young King and for the civil disobedience movement.

Martin Luther King's activities later took on national dimensions, especially when he was placed at the head of hundreds of thousands of citizens – black and white – in a march on Washington on 28 August 1963. There, from the steps of the Lincoln Memorial, he made his famous 'I have a dream' speech.

> 'Go back to Mississippi,' said King to the people gathered, 'go back to Alabama, go back to South Carolina, go back to Louisiana, go back to wherever there are huts and ghettos in North America and spread the hope of radical change.'

He gained international recognition in 1964 when he was awarded the Nobel Prize for Peace. In 1965, the struggles of the civil rights movement came to fruition when a law was passed in the US Congress that recognised African-American citizens' right to vote without limitations, of which those in many southern states had been deprived until then.

A source of inspiration for King was Mahatma Gandhi, leader of the independence movement in India who, with his non-violent actions, shook the British colonial regime to its foundations, leading to the independence of his great country in 1947.

King said that a true revolution of values would make us wonder about the justice of many of our past and present policies. A true revolution in values would permit no complacency in dealing with the yawning gap between rich and poor. The arrogance of Westerners, who believe that we have everything to teach others and nothing to learn from them, he said, is unfair.

At King's side on the Washington march were white Americans from the fields of academia, art and the trade unions, among whom was the actor Marlon Brando who wrote that he was standing just 'a few steps behind Dr King, when he gave his "I have a dream" speech', and that the sound of his words still echoed in his mind.

King's efforts in favour of non-violence and civil disobedience as forms of action continued the long tradition of such movements in the US. Comparable methods were likewise used by the great English peace activist, author and philosopher, Bertrand Russell. Born in 1872, Russell opposed World War One from the outset, and took an active part in the movement of No Conscription into the British Army, which cost him his job as lecturer at Cambridge University. He was then offered a post at Harvard but the British authorities refused him a passport to travel to the USA.

Nehru

In 1918, he was sentenced to six months in jail and found himself in Brixton prison, where he wrote an anti-militarist article for the newspaper *Tribunal*. While in prison, he also wrote much of his book *An Introduction to Mathematical Philosophy*, which he completed the following year. His anti-war views did not stop him supporting the anti-Hitler alliance in World War Two, recognising the anti-fascist nature of this war. After World War Two, he was among the first to denounce the nuclear holocausts of Hiroshima and Nagasaki, and joined the fight for the full abolition of nuclear weapons.

Sukarno

The view adopted by Labour Party conferences (even during the Cold War) in favour of Britain's unilateral nuclear disarmament owes much to Russell and to many others who held the same beliefs. The heralds of anti-Sovietism and supporters of the doctrine of nuclear deterrence then adopted the slogan 'Better Dead then Red', which Russell and his fellow campaigners reversed to 'Better Red than Dead'.

II
The Non-Aligned Movement

There was a significant development in the pursuit of peace when the Movement of Non-Aligned Countries was established in 1955 at a conference of 29 states in Bandung, Indonesia, upon an initiative by the Prime Minister of India, Pandit Nehru, and Presidents Sukarno of Indonesia, Nasser of Egypt, and Tito of Yugoslavia. Einstein sent greetings to the conference in Bandung; the reading of his message coincided with the news that this great scientist and champion of peace had died.

The criteria and principles for membership in the

Nasser

Tito

movement were set out in a preparatory meeting in Cairo (5-12 June 1961) prior to its first Summit Conference in Belgrade later the same year. They were:
1. Independent and non-aligned foreign policy based on peaceful co-existence.
2. Consistent support for national liberation movements.
3. Non-participation in military pacts or regional military alliances.
4. A country seeking admission must have no foreign military bases on its soil.

This was followed by the first Summit Conference in Belgrade in September 1961, which was attended by Archbishop Makarios, President of Cyprus, signifying the membership of the newly constituted Republic of Cyprus. This was viewed with profound suspicion by Britain and the US, and later prompted them to describe Makarios as the 'Fidel Castro of the Mediterranean'.

Membership in the Non-Aligned Movement increased as the colonial era came to an end, and its international presence became more marked through its initiatives to democratise the UN and prevent it from being manipulated by the great powers, to bridge the north-south gap in the world through a New International Economic Order, and to abolish the debt of developing countries.

III
The Cuba Crisis – Unarmed Victory

In October 1962, humanity hovered on the brink of a nuclear war between the USA and the USSR over the Cuban Missile Crisis. The crisis lasted for about 13 days.

The revolution had triumphed in Cuba on 1 January 1959, under the leadership of Fidel Castro and Che Guevara, who overthrew the corrupt Batista dictatorship. The US leadership could not stomach the new reality and started making plans for a military intervention in Cuba. As early as 1961, a landing in the Bay of Pigs was organised, ostensibly by anti-Castro Cubans living in Miami. The Bay of Pigs operation has gone down in history as a humiliating fiasco for the Kennedy administration. The crisis culminated on 23 October 1962 with the US blockade of Cuba.

At these very crucial moments for the future of mankind, Bertrand Russell was spurred into action: his interventions were described as decisive by many contemporary newspapers. Robert Kennedy, too, in his memoir of these events, entitled *Thirteen Days*, believed it was his obligation to include Russell's telegram to President John F. Kennedy. Russell himself collected his efforts in this regard in a book entitled *Unarmed Victory*.

Although there may be some who disputed or underestimated the significance of Russell's interventions, one cannot ignore the fact that the English philosopher had warned of the dangerous escalation of the tension surrounding Cuba in his statement of 3 September 1962, in which he said that the situation in Cuba boded a serious threat to peace in the world. The Cubans had every right to the government they wanted and, even if it was a communist government, under no circumstances could US intervention be justified. If the US invaded Cuba, it could provoke military action by the USSR. The situation required a decisive commitment by the US government not to invade Cuba, and by the Soviet Union not to arm Cuba.

On 18 October, Russell sent a telegram to the UN Secretary General U Thant, asking for permission to address the General Assembly. After Kennedy's announcement of the Cuban blockade, Russell sent five telegrams to Kennedy and Khrushchev.

Russell's interventions to end the crisis were extolled in an editorial in *Roads of Peace* (November 1962), featuring his photograph on the cover with the caption 'Help Preserve the Peace'. The editorial said, among other things:

Bertrand Russell

'There was something profoundly moving about the dialogue between the philosopher and the two heads of state during the most acute stage of the crisis … As these lines are being written, people are breathing more easily. We have moved away from the edge of a cliff, and now, after the chill of fear, the time has come for reflection … So Peace has been preserved. First victory. The situation in Cuba has stabilised. Second victory. The 'exiled' Cubans in the US and their rabid supporters have understood this very well, which was why they were not cheering in triumph, but making cantankerous and evasive statements … '

Finally, the crisis led to a re-examination of all international problems. The test ban and the abolition of bases in foreign countries became issues on the agenda for the first time.

In the same issue, under the headline 'Fear', the poet Nikiforos Vrettakos wrote in his monthly column:

'Let me go straight to 23 October 1962, when the fear of an unprecedented catastrophe cast its shadow over our entire planet. It was the blockade of Cuba and the anguish in the hearts of billions of people over the yellow radioactivity that was threatening to sweep the greater part of the globe indiscriminately. This was the greatest fear to have gripped humankind since the world began, fear of the terrifying danger that man himself had created, a fear that made all other fears look childish by comparison.'

As in all the rest of the world, public opinion in Greece experienced the same anguish over the Cuba crisis, and mobilised for peace. In the issue of *Roads of Peace* mentioned earlier, a text was published entitled: 'Appeal by public figures: LET PEACE BE SAVED', with the magazine's introductory note:

'At the most critical stage of the recent international crisis, it is no exaggeration to say that the entire Greek people, irrespective of their political convictions, stood decisively united in their opinion that Greece must stay far away from war and in their decision to do everything possible to preserve the peace. It is characteristic that dozens of outstanding public figures, politicians, scientists and people of the arts and letters, representing the most highly divergent opinions, addressed the following appeal to the competent Greek authorities:

Anxiety and fear grip all of humanity in face of the dangerously escalating situation caused by the blockade of Cuba. Never before have we been so close to war. Never before has human civilisation been at such great risk. Greece, too, is threatened with total annihilation. Calm, the spirit of national unity, and devotion to the cause of peace must distinguish the leadership of this country and the Greek people. From this small corner of the earth, we express our opposition to any offensive action, whatever its origin, that will lead to the extinction of the human race, and we believe that our country must also contribute to the success of relevant international initiatives. With high morale and a sense of responsibility, we address an appeal to all competent authorities to keep our country away from any deadly adventure, to ensure its survival and normalcy in our national life.'

Later in the 1960s, Russell was also responsible for organising an informal international tribunal to try the US for war crimes committed in Vietnam. Similar autonomous projects continue, such as the Russell Tribunal on Palestine, in this case with the support of the Bertrand Russell Peace Foundation, which has its headquarters in Nottingham, England.

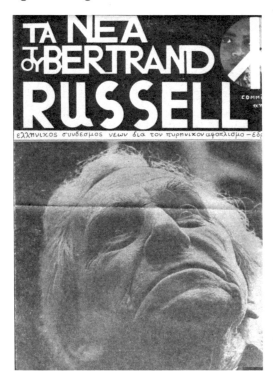

CHAPTER 4

Lambrakis and Peace

I

In the Forefront of the Movement

*He saw the goal: 'Peace. Peace for Greece. Peace for the world.
Peace for man, animals, plants. All of life in brotherhood before
the direct threat.'*

Nikiforos Vrettakos

Nikiforos Vrettakos used these all-embracing words about the peace movement – long before the modern ecologists – in an epitaph he wrote for Grigoris Lambrakis in June 1963.

Lambrakis' involvement in the peace movement had begun in 1958, as a founding member of the Greek Committee for Balkan Understanding. The following year, in his capacity as member of this Committee, he gave a lecture on 'the role of sport in the peaceful co-existence of the peoples'.

Grigoris was already actively involved in politics, helping his brother Thodoros who, in 1956, was elected Deputy for Piraeus representing the Democratic Union party. Tragically, Thodoros died suddenly of heart failure a few months later. Grigoris did not run in the next parliamentary elections in 1958, but went to Tripoli to help his cousin Odysseas Tsoukopoulos, who was a candidate on the United Democratic Left (EDA) ballot.

In the 1961 parliamentary elections, Lambrakis was on the ballot of PAME (EDA and collaborating candidates) in the First District of Piraeus and was elected Deputy; he came second to Antonis Brillakis[1] in the number of votes received. Among his papers, a draft entitled 'First speech' was found scribbled on a sheet torn from his prescription pad. It was part of his first election campaign speech:

'Dear friends, I am campaigning in these elections with two main objectives: peace and democracy. We want peace so that no missile bases are built and Greece is not destroyed. We want peace so we can have friendly relations with the peoples of our neighbouring Balkan countries. And we want real democracy so that there is equality; equality before the law and justice for all citizens irrespective of their political views. We want democracy so that there is at last recognition for the finest achievement of the Greek people – our heroic National Resistance against the German-Italian fascists and their local collaborators.'

*Lambrakis' parliamentary
election campaign poster*

The status of Deputy brought Lambrakis into the front ranks of the peace movement. On 19 March 1962, he took part in the Europe-wide preparatory conference in Vienna for the World Conference for General Disarmament to be held in Moscow. On 7 May 1962, he was the keynote speaker, together with professor Kostas Tzonis, at a rally of the Labour Movement for Disarmament and Peace. Among other things, he said:

> 'Crisis, dead end, delay – the same words keep being repeated, and we keep dancing around in the same dance of Zalongo.[2] Wealthy Greece, under-developed Greece. Cradle of civilisation, but with thousands of illiterate citizens and schools in ruins. Greece with schools but no teachers. Greece with teachers but no jobs. Year after year, military spending keeps increasing, even though it is already among the highest in Europe … Friends, workers, employees, intellectuals, farmers, we must all mobilise together for disarmament and peace.'

On 4 June 1962, *Roads of Peace* held a meeting about the Aldermaston march at which Markos Dragoumis and Professor Kostas Tzonis spoke.

In the same year, after EEDYE's first national conference on peace and disarmament on 24 June, Lambrakis was elected Vice-President. The themes of the conference were the Greek and International Peace Movement, Disarmament and Peace, and a Nuclear-free Balkans. The conference re-elected Andreas Zakkas as EEDYE President.

The next landmark for Lambrakis was the World Conference in Moscow (9-14 July 1962) which he attended as a member of the EEDYE delegation. He took the floor in one of the working groups at the conference and, according to a report in the EEDYE bulletin of the time, said:

> 'We have come to Moscow, the capital of this great socialist country, not to take part in an offensive alliance, but to make ourselves available for fruitful discussions about achieving disarmament and peace. The most characteristic feature of our conference is the fact that people with different national, racial and class origins are taking part. We have found a common language in which to discuss the most burning issues of our era, with the most humanitarian and civilised slogans: disarmament and peace, and to chart a common path for the peoples to follow in order to achieve them. We make a heartfelt appeal to all peoples to face the threat of nuclear war honestly, with a profound sense of responsibility. Thus, the most urgent issue is to end nuclear testing in the atmosphere, on land and at sea, as these tests will certainly be disastrous to the health of the human race.
>
> We know that the atomic bombs dropped on Hiroshima and Nagasaki killed 150,000 Japanese, and that thousands more were affected by radioactivity and died later, and that people are still dying from it. Pregnant women miscarried, developed malignant tumours, leukaemia, serious damage to their reproductive organs, incurable skin disorders, etc.
>
> The physicians in the Greek delegation feel fortunate that they are collaborating with doctors from other countries at this world conference on disarmament and peace in Moscow, and believe that we are proceeding towards peace, so that human beings

can live without wars and without fears. The Greek people want general disarmament and peace, and are fighting for denuclearised zones to be created, especially in the Balkan peninsula where they live.'

II
Lambrakis at Aldermaston

Peace marches traditionally took place in Western European countries at Easter; the best known of these was the march organised by the Campaign for Nuclear Disarmament (CND) in Britain, in 1958, from the atomic research facility at Aldermaston to London. At the time, CND had only recently been formed, but attained international participation none the less.

In 1961, the Greek peace movement was represented by Giannis Theodorakis and, in 1962, by Markos Dragoumis. The latter, editor-in-chief of *Roads of Peace*, closed his extensive report of the march – entitled 'We, 150,000 marchers for Peace, are walking to London'– in the May 1962 issue with these words:

'Leaving England, I said goodbye to our good friend Owen Mortimer, who said something that was both very plain but also very serious. "Next year," he said, "I will come to the Aldermaston march that you're going to organise in Greece".'

This indicates that discussion of the Marathon March began in 1962. On 4-7 January 1963, Lambrakis took part in an international conference organised by CND in Oxford. It was reported by *Roads of Peace* in January 1963:

'Deputy Grigoris Lambrakis took part in the Conference as representative of the Greek Peace Committee, and contributed to the work of its plenary session and to various committees. Upon his proposal, the following were discussed: the creation of a missile-free zone in the Balkans, the concern of the Cretan people about the bases deployed on Crete, and the tough conditions under which the peace movement is

(left to right) Leonidas Kyrkos at the Aldermaston march with a Buddhist monk, Manolis Glezos and Grigoris Lambrakis

growing in Greece. He asked that help be provided by the delegations of European peace movements for the possible organisation of a peace march in Greece at Easter.'

On 11 April 1963, the board of EEDYE convened and arrived at two significant decisions: 1) that it be represented by Grigoris Lambrakis at the Aldermaston-London Peace March, and 2) that it take part in the Marathon Peace March that was already being planned by the Bertrand Russell League.

Greek participants in the Aldermaston March in 1963 were Grigoris Lambrakis, Manolis Glezos, Leonidas Kyrkos, Spyros Linardatos and Betty Ambatielou, together with Greek students and workers in England as well as many members of the large Cypriot community there. Lambrakis kept a diary about this exciting event.

'I arrived in London the evening before the march. It was Holy Thursday. I went to the County Hotel where I found room 416 in which Glezos and Kyrkos were staying. I left a note on the door saying that I had arrived for the march and then fell asleep. At midnight, Manolis knocked at the door and hugged me. "I'm going to get Leonidas." And they arrived. I gave them a package of cigarettes, some pistachios and today's Greek newspapers. They looked through them anxiously, and told me that we had to get up at 6:30 the next morning, Good Friday, for the drive to Aldermaston where the march was going to start.

"First will be the Japanese," Manolis told me, "because of Hiroshima. They'll be followed by the Greek delegation."

"Because of Manolis Glezos," I said.

Manolis lowered his head and did not reply … They left and promised to give me a wake up call next morning. Like a kid from a village, I couldn't sleep for worrying about the march.'

Then, in his personal diary, Lambrakis wrote a report of the march:

'We left London at 8am for Aldermaston. There was a general alert in London about the march. The roads in that direction were packed.

At 12 noon, we entered Aldermaston where there is a British base that builds atomic bombs. There's also an American base. This is why the protest march is starting from here.

Time: 12:15. Thousands of peace-marchers standing on threshing floors overgrown with weeds beside the nuclear base, with black placards bearing the name of each country, the peace symbol and slogans against the bases, etc. Orchestras were playing. People of all races and colours. A group of Cypriots are singing one of Mikis' songs with a group of Spaniards. On one banner is written:

How long will we walk?
Four days.
Is that all?

Cypriots and young people from all countries are gazing at the enormous delegations and collecting signatures to send by the thousands to Karamanlis, asking him to allow the Marathon Peace March. Everybody is holding a black banner and black flags with slogans about peace and disarmament. Canon Collins' voice is heard constantly announcing slogans from the loudspeaker.

On the 1963 Aldermaston march

The Greeks march in second place in the international section of the march, which is headed by the delegation from Hiroshima. After us (four) came the Cypriots (one hundred). The procession at this moment was 6 km long, and we were still at the start. One slogan read: "Fight wars with books not bombs".

Among the Japanese from Hiroshima who were walking ahead of us is a man in yellow, beating a drum rhythmically and chanting a dirge very sadly for the 200,000 who were killed by the bomb. By beating the drum and chanting the dirge he kept saying: "I am the truth and I pray for Peace in the world". His right arm was not covered, and as he beat the drum you could see a scar as big as the palm of your hand from the bombing of Hiroshima.

Food: bread and olives and marching ...

On one placard was written: "A weapon-free world can be a hunger-free world"...

Hundreds of families were pushing their children in prams and pushchairs and walking them down the road of peace. Very moving sight.

At 4 there was a rest stop in a forest. We were given bread, olives and a coffee.

At 4:15pm we started out again. Now it is 6:30 and we continue our march. We have arrived at the end of the first day's march in the city of Reading (population 150,000) after 15,000 peace-loving people, spread over a distance of 6 kilometres, walked 19,200 metres.

Public figures taking part included Labour MPs Arthur Greenwood, Michael Foot and Sydney Silverman; John Bernal, President of the World Peace Council, Canon John Collins of St Paul's Cathedral, Stanley Evans ...

SECOND DAY

Distance of 32 km from Reading (note: the city of Reading is also known for the progressive poem by Oscar Wilde, "The Ballad of Reading Gaol") to Slough under heavy rain. A group of 2,000 pacifists marched through a camp of one of the "regional seats of government" (which will assume the governance of whatever remains of the country after a nuclear war). Some 3,000 pacifists marched into the camp and observed a minute's silence; eight people stayed there for 24 hours.'

He added on a separate slip of paper:

'Second day. People everywhere applauded. They were sleeping in tents and houses appropriated. It was very cold. A route of 32 km (20 miles). Banners proclaiming the brotherhood of Cyprus and Greece. The most cheerful delegation.

THIRD DAY

We started at 8:30 in the morning from Slough … Along the way in the rain we walked 5,000 metres; people kept joining the march enthusiastically, especially young people. Lots of orchestras. Today four people came from West Germany despite the ban.

FOURTH DAY

Outside London.

There's an enormous banner here showing a dinosaur, on which is written: "The Dinosaur was armed by nature like a lobster. But with a small brain he became extinct"…

At the starting point on the Green Coast, there are 300,000 people.

Song of the Cypriots: "Our war will be different. There won't be swords and cannons."

We continue on through London on our way to Hyde Park. Yesterday, the circulation of *Sanity* (a pacifist newspaper) was banned. Today, it circulated illegally and I got a copy.

I've been holding the banner with the words *GREECE* – throughout the four days of the march, together with Deputy Leonidas Kyrkos. When we arrived at the statue of Lord Byron, Glezos had the inspired idea that we should all go (stepping out of the march for 2 minutes) and sing our National Anthem. We went and sang the Anthem twice …

In London the march was 30km long. The head reached Hyde Park at 3pm, and the last marchers from 8pm onwards. Enthusiasm, celebration, singing and speeches in Hyde Park. Collins, the leader of the march, spoke; the priest said he had walked 50-60 km. Then Manolis Glezos embraced Collins.'

Here Lambrakis' report of the march in his diary ends, but he never stopped recording his impressions, full of child-like enthusiasm, in his effort to retain these unique experiences of hope in his memory.

III
Return to London: Betty Ambatielou

On 26 April 1963, Grigoris Lambrakis made another trip to London. It happened that Queen Frederika of Greece was also there on a private visit.[3] As Parliamentary Deputy, he wanted to help arrange a meeting between Queen

Frederika and Betty Ambatielou, who wanted to hand Queen Frederika a petition for the release of her husband, the political prisoner Antonis Ambatielos. Even though eleven years had passed since the end of the Civil War in Greece, there were still 1,192 political prisoners.

In London, Lambrakis made the following statement:

Betty Ambatielou waiting for Queen Frederika in London

'I have come to London to ask Queen Frederika to agree to see Mrs Ambatielou, because it is now known that neither the Parliament nor even the Government are ruling Greece, but Queen Frederika. Unfortunately the Queen refused to see me, even though, as a parliamentary deputy, I represent the Greek people. I would like to warn the Queen that her policy will lead the Throne to disaster...'[4]

Lambrakis' effort found no response, which was hardly surprising, given the Palace's negative attitude towards the desire for national reconciliation. This attitude was maintained by King Paul's successor on the throne, his son Constantine, who in his 1966 New Year message described communists as 'poison'.

In October 1945, a League for Democracy in Greece (LDG) was active in Britain. Its goals included a general amnesty for all democratic Greek political prisoners and the restoration of trade union and political liberties. This organisation was strongly supported by the powerful British unions, and developed broad actions during the Civil War in Greece and in the years afterwards, as well as against the junta from 1967 to 1974.

In 1961, during Greek Prime Minister Konstantinos Karamanlis' visit to London, the League organised a protest demonstration at which the main speaker was Betty Ambatielou. She had broken the police cordon around Karamanlis and the British officials who welcomed him, holding a poster on which was written 'Give me my husband back', an image that was featured on the front page of many newspapers the next day.

During her visit, Queen Frederika stayed at the five-star Claridge's Hotel in London. Lambrakis had sought an audience with her on behalf of Betty Ambatielou, to promote the release of her husband and other political prisoners. As noted earlier, the Queen refused to receive him. Meanwhile, many protesters had gathered outside Claridge's, including Cypriot and Greek communists living in London, as well as British trade unionists. To avoid the protesters, Frederika left the hotel through the side door. Mrs Ambatielou saw her and approached her to give her the letter, but did not lay a hand on her, as was misleadingly reported in the press, especially in Greece.

The events in London preoccupied the Parliament of the Hellenes in its session of 8 May 1963, when Lambrakis took the floor to defend Betty Ambatielou with these words:

'Mr Speaker, Mrs Ambatielou showed courtesy, not violence as was written in the press. I went to London in an effort to get her message to Queen Frederika through the Crown Prince's aide, but he refused to accept it. The British television and press met with Mrs Ambatielou, who explained that it was not her intention to make trouble for Queen Frederika, but to ask her aide to pass on the petition. She said that lies were written about her as she created no episode. The role of Mrs Ambatielou was a role in support of democracy, it was a national role.'

With these words Lambrakis stirred up trouble for himself. He had crossed the reactionary and fanatical forces. He had become a 'red flag' to the parastate.

Footnotes
1. Antonis Brillakis had been active in the resistance against the Nazis and the junta. He was a founding member of the Communist Party of the Interior. He was elected as a Parliamentary Deputy eight times.
2. In 1803, facing imminent capture by Ottoman soldiers and death or slavery, a group of families from Souli in northern Greece sought refuge on top of the Zalongo cliff. All died, and 22 women danced to their death.
3. In July of the same year, King Paul and Queen Frederika were scheduled to make a state visit to England. Greek Prime Minister Konstantinos Karamanlis had advised the royal couple against the trip because of possible protests, but Frederika insisted on going ahead with it. Karamanlis proved to have been right. As Michael Randle reported:
   'On 7 July the Campaign for Nuclear Disarmament (CND) organised a silent march from the Byron statue at Hyde Park Corner in tribute to Lambrakis. On 9 July, the ad hoc "Save Greece Now Committee" – of which the Committee of 100 were members – organised a march from Trafalgar Square to Buckingham Palace, at which 94 people were arrested. I took part in that demonstration and saw the violence the police used in trying to suppress it. In one incident I witnessed, they rode their horses into the demonstrators on the pavement.'
4. G. Voultepsis, *The Lambrakis Case* (in Greek), Vol I, p. 74.

CHAPTER 5

The Greek May of 1963

I
The First Marathon Peace March

Holding Greece in your open arms
you flew up
the tumulus steps; you did not descend
but rather ascended.

Yannis Ritsos

Lambrakis returned to Athens for the march from Marathon to Athens, or 'the Greek Aldermaston' as it was sometimes called. Marathon has become the worldwide symbol of the toughest endurance race. It was initially the joyous setting for the victory of a few Athenians over countless invading Persians, a landmark in the evolution of humankind. But above all, the victory at Marathon was a moral victory. It destroyed the myth of the invincible Medes, and revealed that democracy can produce capable military and political leaders, and ensure a battle-worthy army; that it can resist internal friction and secure long-term peace. Since 1963, Marathon has also signified Lambrakis.

The proposed march was banned by the Karamanlis Government early in April, to the extent that a campaign against the march had even been orchestrated; announcements by non-existent organisations such as the 'Democratic Peace Institute' and the 'Movement for Freedom and Democratic Peace' said they would 'defend the sanctity of Marathon (10.4.1963). A few days later, banners started appearing in the region bearing slogans such as 'No to the Communist Marathon March' and 'To Russell and his followers: Hands off the sacred soil of Marathon'.

On his return from London, Lambrakis visited the Bertrand Russell Youth League office in Athens on 16 April, and handed over a petition bearing the signatures of thousands of Aldermaston marchers in favour of the Marathon march. He had also brought with him the banner bearing the emblem of disarmament with the word ΕΛΛΑΣ on one side and *GREECE* on the other.

The delegation from the British peace movement was headed by Dr John Chambers, who had arrived on Tuesday 16 April for the march, and the next day requested (unsuccessfully) a meeting with Prime

Pamphlet about the first Marathon March

Michalis Peristerakis speaking in 1963

Minister Konstantinos Karamanlis. The right-wing government did not back down, but nor did the organisers of the march.

At a press conference on 18 April, Michalis Peristerakis, President of the Russell Youth League, insisted that the march would take place, and denounced the hostile climate and terrorist methods used by the police in their efforts to cancel the march. Many British peace activists were present at the press conference. On the eve of the march, four of them were arrested and deported.

On 19 April, the organisers complained that coach rental for the march was being hindered, and proposed that those who were unable to reach the starting point of the Mound of Marathon make the march in the opposite direction, from Athens to Marathon. Everything was ready for this popular event. Mikis Theodorakis had already written his:

Song for the March

From Marathon we started out
To Athens we were heading.
Why don't you come too?
Come along with us.
Let's bind the sun forever
to our beloved Greece.
With a handshake we vowed
to save the Peace we vowed.
We dreamed of work, dance, and song
To bind the sun we dreamed
To save the world we vowed.
Come along with us.

The issue of *Avgi* published on the eve of the march ran the front-page banner headline: 'ERE fears the Marathon march'.

And so, on the morning of 21 April 1963, when Lambrakis set out on his march from the Mound of Marathon, Michalis Peristerakis, Russell's secretary Pat Pottle, and hundreds of others started from the *Stegi Patridos* (*Homeland House*), in the central Athens district of Ambelokipi, for the walk to Marathon. However, just a few hundred metres down the road, they found themselves face-to-face with the police. '2,000 arrested for defying Government ban' was the smaller headline in the British newspaper *Peace News* on 26 April, over the main banner headline 'Greek march success'.

Typical of the attitude of the right-wing press was the caption in *Mesimvrini* (22.4) under the photograph of Lambrakis marching: 'Marcher, wretched and alone'. The headline, however, was belied by the accompanying text about 10,000 policemen lining the route, which suggested that there were thousands of marchers.

Arrests had begun in the preceding days, including those of foreign representatives – mainly from Britain – who had come for the march. John Chambers, head of the British delegation (representing CND and Committee of 100), had arrived in Athens with his wife Judy. They were followed by the MP Malcolm Macmillan (third from right in photo above), Pat Pottle, John Petherbridge, Jennifer Homer and M. Cossuta from Italy.

Two days before the March, on Friday 19 April, six policemen arrested Chambers and most of the British delegation, kept them at General Security and freed them that same evening. The next day, five policemen arrested them again in the office of the Russell Youth League and brought them to the Aliens' Bureau. From there at 6:30 in the evening they were taken to a shack on the edge of Hellenikon Airport, from where they were taken to the departure gate at 4:45am to be deported. They left for London at 5:05am as the first Greek marchers were heading towards Marathon.

Pat Pottle, at least, was able to appear in

Pat Pottle in Greece

Ambelokipi on the Sunday morning for the reverse Athens-to-Marathon march. Then, as he described in *Peace News*, four lorries arrived and arrested him and others. They took him to the Police Station, and then to the Athens Police Chief, whose only phrase in English seems to have been 'Soon to London, then to Moscow'. Three policemen drove Pottle to the airport and put him on a plane.

Mikis Theodorakis, Minos Argyrakis and others went very early in the morning to Ambelokipi for the start of the march, which had been planned by the Russell Youth League. Argyrakis wrote:

'We could see the police vans in the distance, with the police ready to step in. Even though we sat down to avoid being arrested, the police chief suddenly came along and stopped in front of Mikis. Threatening him, he told him to get into the van immediately. So we soon found ourselves with others in the Averoff prison. After quite a long time, we were transferred to a playing field at the end of Patission Street. Among us were Theodorakis, Peristerakis, Alekos Alexandrakis and Argyrakis. When they searched me, they found in my pocket some invitations to a production of the Ugo Betti play *Our dreams* (*I nostri sogni*), for which I had designed the sets. The premiere was to be held the following week. 'Ahaaaa!' shouted the interrogator looking at the invitations. 'They are confiscated. They represent evidence and documentation of the tricks and conspiratorial measures you reds use!'

Shielded by his parliamentary position, Lambrakis managed to get through the police cordons, one by one, in his car. At the beginning he was accompanied by his wife Roula, Ioulia Linardatou, and the Cypriot poet Tefkros Anthias, who had come from London for the march. But at the Rafina turn-off the police made the

Peace News reports

others get out of the car, and Grigoris continued alone.

8am. When Lambrakis arrived at the Mound, he passed rapidly among the policemen. A woman named Euphrosyne Polychroni took advantage of the confusion to ascend and place a few flowers reverently on the tumulus, making the point that women everywhere are in the front ranks of the cause of peace, and that they have always safeguarded peace, from Lysistrata to the present day. She was followed immediately by Lambrakis. He walked up the Mound, and as he was coming down he unfurled a black banner (the one he held at Aldermaston) with white letters spelling a highly subversive slogan, the word ΕΛΛΑΣ *(GREECE)*, flanked on the right and left by the emblem of nuclear disarmament, the symbol of peace.

'Long Live Peace, Long Live Democracy,' shouted Lambrakis with his stentorian voice. At that moment, the Greek people had joined the peace march symbolically.

As soon as the gendarmes recovered from their surprise they rushed up to take the banner from him, while a few hot-headed types shouted war cries. Lambrakis resisted. 'This banner is sacred,' he shouted. 'You have no right to take it.'

For half an hour this unarmed man struggled with a gang of gendarmes for possession of the banner. He got it, unfolded the precious trophy and marched on with it, shouting 'Long live peace!'

At Nea Makri Lambrakis was joined by three others who appear in a photograph that was published in many newspapers and is still being used: Andreas Goutis from Kokkinia (whose brother Kostas was a fellow athlete and friend of Lambrakis), Andreas Mammonas and Babis Papadopoulos. They got as far as the Rafina intersection, where fifty policemen hastened to grab the banner. Once again Lambrakis resisted, until the banner began to tear. Later he said: 'They didn't take it from me. I handed it to them.'

In fact, he handed it to the Rafina gendarmerie so that it would not be damaged; some parastate thugs had gathered and shortly thereafter grabbed him, as police and reporters looked on. But in the end Grigoris got away and continued with a few marchers accompanying him. The reporters followed them and were pestered by the police, who did not want publicity for this march.

They arrived at Pikermi at around 10am. Lambrakis asked the officer in charge if they could lay a few flowers on the graves of the patriots who were executed by the Germans. He did not refuse, but some gendarmes grabbed the flowers and scattered them about, cursing and swearing. Lambrakis and those following him observed a minute's silence in memory of those lost in the cause of Greece's freedom.

After 10am the gendarmes arrested the few remaining marchers around him and kept the reporters at bay. Lambrakis continued alone. He had walked 14 km. Then they arrested him on orders from the public prosecutor.

'You are under arrest because a felony may be committed,' an officer of the law told him before shoving him into the patrol car.

'Felony? By whom? Against whom?'

They kept him for three hours. As he was leaving, dusty and harassed, a plainclothesman asked him: 'Is it possible that you don't have any money, and that's why you're doing all this?'

'You poor man,' replied Lambrakis. 'I make a lot of money from my work. But I'm fighting for peace and justice. I'm fighting for you, too!'

A while later he was in the office of the Peace Committee sending telegrams which read: 'The desire of our democratic people for a Marathon-Athens Peace March has been realised.'

The next day, the photograph of Lambrakis with the banner open – like a swallow ready to take flight, like the Cross – went round the world. Marathon again marked a new global victory for peace.

On 22 April, the newspaper *Athinaiki* wrote under banner headlines:

'YESTERDAY THE GOVERNMENT WAGED WAR (not against the Turks but) AGAINST THE ADVOCATES OF PEACE. 2,000 CITIZENS ARRESTED (Alexandrakis, Georgouli, Theodorakis, Argyrakis).
'Those attacked by police included: President of the Russell Youth League, Pat Pottle, reporters, photographers, and one hundred others, Greeks and foreigners. Finally, the Deputy Gr. Lambrakis ascended the Mound of Marathon.'

On the contrary, the main headline in the right-wing *Vradyni* was: 'Marathon March a dismal failure'. Featured on its front page was the banner hung in Marathon by far-right extremists, on which was written: 'Communists out of Marathon!'.

The main theme in *Ta Nea* the day after was the anti-march stance of the (right-wing) ERE government under the headline: 'Panic measures used by Government to deal with the Marchers. Many foreigners deported.'

The news of Lambrakis' march, the arrests and deportations of foreigners went around the world. On 22 April, Alekos Alexandrakis, Minos Argyrakis, Aliki Georgouli and Mikis Theodorakis gave a press conference. In the evening, the organisers of the March held a rally. The Acropol theatre was packed with people who wanted to hear from Grigoris Lambrakis, Mikis Theodorakis and Michalis Peristerakis; to hear that the peace movement had entered a new stage of growth after the March. By banning the march and resorting to intimidation, the government had achieved precisely the opposite of what it intended.

II
Lambrakis reports to Parliament about the March

On Wednesday 24 April, during a scheduled parliamentary debate, the issue was raised of police violence during the first Marathon Peace March. During the debate, Lambrakis took the floor. It was to be his last major speech in Parliament,

Betty Ambatielou

other than intervening briefly on behalf of Betty Ambatielou on 8 May. The following excerpts provide his first-hand account of what happened on the March.

'Honorable Deputies of Parliament, I am profoundly distressed because the Speaker of the House, who has sworn to defend the Constitution, violated it this evening when, through his words, he essentially approved of my unconstitutional arrest for taking part in the peace march from Marathon to Athens. In this way, of course, the amendment of the Constitution is justified. So far, a Deputy of this House has been brutally manhandled three times by the security police, and even though the Speaker of the House was informed, he took no steps. Speaking today, the Deputy Prime Minister expressed his esteem for me. I, too, would like to assure the Deputy Prime Minister of my esteem for him and, I might add, my respect. Nevertheless, despite the fact that he concerned himself with the matter, he said and did nothing about my arrest and abduction by organs of the law and my criminal mistreatment.

The Deputy Prime Minister said that he saw my photograph in the newspapers and observed elation in my face. In fact, my face looked elated because he knew what I was doing. I had arrived at the Mound of Marathon, a symbol of war, to raise my voice in favour of changing the symbols of war to symbols of peace and love. And when I was at the top of the Mound, the foot of it was surrounded by hundreds of armed gendarmes …

When I was on the Mound, I had the impression that the men who had fallen in battle, fighting for the independence of Greece, would have shouted with me 'No more War, but Peace'. At that same moment, a gendarme shouted 'Down with Peace' and when I told the Commander that this man should be arrested, there was no response. Finally, thanks to my effort and his courage, the police were withdrawn and I started on the road to Athens.

I walked to the Rafina intersection where Captain F. Tzoumanis of the gendarmerie, accompanied by about 30 gendarmes and three thugs, arrested me as I was holding the precious banner from the Aldermaston March, which in the end, half an hour later, they succeeded in taking from me. After they mauled and humiliated me, I contined my march with five other peace activists and arrived at the Tumulus of those executed by the Fascists and Nazis at Pikermi. There I placed a few flowers on the Mound, only to see Major A. Vradis stomp on them. And while I was observing a moment's silence, they were pushing me.

Despite all the above, I continued on my way. And now I would like to ask what precisely was my crime? At the 30th kilometre, Lieutenant-Colonel Pistolis and Major Vradis ordered me to stop. I refused. Then Mr. Vardoulakis and Mr. Tomaras came by and gave the order to arrest me.

In the presence and by order of Pistolis and Vradis, and led by Warrant Officer Ioannis Leotsarakos, I was arrested, tossed into a truck like a sack of potatoes, and accompanied by eight truncheon-bearing gendarmes. If you didn't know I was a Parliamentary Deputy you'd have thought they were taking me off to be executed. Then I was sent to Nea Makri and afterwards to Marathon. From there, I was driven through the mountain villages of Souli, Grammatikos, Kapandritis and Tatoi, and abandoned in Nea Ionia after three-and-a-half very uncomfortable hours. On the way I talked to the gendarmes about peace, and Leotsarakos replied as follows: 'What do you want with all this? Democracy is miserable. Yes, we want war.'

A few days ago, it was my honour, fellow Deputies, to take part in the great 80km march from Aldermaston to London. The Minister of Public Security said that anarchists might create episodes here. There were also anarchists on the London march. But the police walked alongside the marchers. When the march reached the Palace gates, some wanted to deviate from the route, but they were subdued. Here, too, the march should be permitted, and if any episodes occur, only then should the law be imposed …

The Government banned the peace march because the meaning of the march is opposed to the policy of the Government. The policy of the Government is bellicose and not based on achieving real peace … Fellow deputies, the Minister of Public Security said that peace marches should take place in countries in which preparations are being made for nuclear war. My view is that peace marches should also take place in countries to which nuclear weapons are supplied. Fellow deputies, it is true that 2,500 years ago in Marathon, Miltiades defeated the Persians. It is also true that the Government, with its truncheon-bearing police and thugs, defeated the peace marchers and true democrats. But the Government knows that we will continue our struggles to establish peace in the world, and for the true meaning of democracy to dawn in our country.'

III
The Assassination

GOTZAMANIS: I've got a job to do tonight, so I won't be able to stop by. Tonight I'm going to do something crazy. To the point of killing a man …

SOTIRHOPOULOS: What are you talking about? Are you serious?

Gotzamanis left in his three-wheeled truck without replying. The decision had been made.

Thessaloniki was destined to become the theatre for the assassination of Grigoris Lambrakis, a month after his triumph at Marathon. The capital city of northern Greece was of special interest to the Right and to the fascist parastate, at a time when the doctrine of the 'danger from the north' was at its height. All sorts of strange organisations were active there, nurtured by Cold War and anti-communist sermons. There, King Paul stated in a speech on 27 October 1957, 'Communism is a transient infectious disease'. It was also where Nikiforidis was executed.

Thousands of pages have been written about the events of 22 May 1963 in Thessaloniki, but one of the best texts is by the editor-in-chief of *Roads of Peace*, Manolis Papoutsakis. We have borrowed it from the archives of this historic magazine:

'The Public Prosecutor and the police were notified in the morning that an execution squad had been organised. Two hundred officers headed by a general and a colonel spent hours watching parastate thugs throwing rocks and breaking windows of the building in which Lambrakis was speaking. They saw people hit Lambrakis and Tsarouchas. They heard his agonised appeals for protection over the loudspeakers. They saw people break the windows of the Red Cross ambulance, take the injured Tsarouchas out and hit him again, seriously injuring him. All the while the gendarmes chatted and joked with the parastate toughs. The hour of the assassins had arrived.

We'll tell you now the story of the crime, and will attempt to represent it based on the evidence that has come to light.

The Thessaloniki Committee for International Détente and Peace organised a rally on Wednesday 22 May

Lambrakis is hit

at 7:30 pm in Piccadilly Hall on Aristotelous Street. Visitors from Athens were to speak at the rally, including Dr. Gr. Lambrakis, assistant professor of medicine, on the theme: 'Peace and disarmament for Greece and for the whole world'. The Committee called all friends of peace to take part in the event.

The announcement was published ten days before the rally. It was to be the first event organised by the Thessaloniki Peace Committee ... Many strange things happened on that fateful day.

On 14 May, two days after the announcement was published, police surveillance of the Thessaloniki Peace Committee began. Lawyer I. Patsas was stalked tirelessly, even to the cemetery where he went to pay his respects at his mother's grave.

Protests by telegram; appeals to all the authorities. The reply: 'There is an order from the Ministry …' For two days, 18 and 19 May, the surveillance ceased; the police were busy protecting General de Gaulle. The members of the parastate organisation National Union – including, of course, Gotzamanis – were called upon by the police to help maintain order in Thessaloniki …

On the evening of 21 May, the day before the rally, the owner of Piccadilly Hall declared his decision not to let the premises, and returned the pre-paid rental.

Wednesday, 22 May dawned … At 10 o'clock in the morning, attorney Sulla Papadimitriou, member of the Thessaloniki Peace Committee, telephoned Public Prosecutor Asimakopoulos to pass on information that a special squad had been formed to assassinate Grigoris Lambrakis. The Prosecutor gave him his reassurances.

At noon, Spyros Gotzamanis, owner and driver of the three-wheeled truck bearing licence number 49981, dropped into the furniture workshop of G. Sotirhopoulos at 10 Georgiou Stavrou Street. They had agreed that Gotzamanis would pick up and deliver some furniture, but when he arrived, Sotirhopoulos told him that the merchandise was not ready, and that he should return in the evening.

At the same time, Lambrakis was arriving at Mikra Airport on an Olympic flight. With him was the second speaker, a lawyer named Rigopoulos. They were met by members of the Thessaloniki Peace Committee, who passed on the news about the surveillance, the hall and the team of assassins. Immediately a representation was made to the police and the Public Prosecutor. The Prosecutor confirmed that he had reported to the police the charges regarding creation of a murder squad …

Finally, at 6pm, another hall was found; the rally would take place in the offices of the Democratic Trade Union Movement, which was on the third floor of a building at the intersection of Ermou and Venizelou, two of the city's main streets, and about 600 metres from Piccadilly Hall.

At 6:30 the rally's change of venue was announced to the police. The officer thanked them, saying that the necessary measures would be taken to keep order …

At 7:00, police in plain clothes and professional 'dissidents' occupied the sidewalks in front of and across from the venue of the rally, joking and chatting in a friendly way.

Gotzamanis took a taxi, licence number 158009 driven by I. Giannatos, and went to the Fifth Police Station, a kilometre away. The taxi waited while Gotzamanis went briefly into the station. He came out accompanied by an unknown person …

At the same time, an announcement by the Peace Committee was posted on the locked door of Piccadilly Hall, informing the public that the rally had changed venue. A plain clothes policeman stood next to it, with an understanding smile.

For 45 minutes, from 7:15 to 8pm, the members of the Peace Committee phoned appeals to the authorities to invoke civil protection: 'Send uniformed policemen to keep order!'

At 8:20, Lambrakis started out from the Cosmopolite Hotel where he was staying for the rally, a distance of 80 metres. He was accompanied by Rigopoulos and Patsas. In front of the entrance to the venue, a parastate thug assailed him and hit him on the head. The police did not so much as lift a finger.

The terrorists were on the offensive, and tried to enter the building, shouting: 'Out with the traitors! Crooks! We're coming to get you!' With difficulty the friends of peace managed to close the iron gate. Rigopoulos stayed outside. The thugs pushed, and tried to open the door …

Lambrakis went up to the third floor. The rally was to begin shortly. The terrorists started throwing rocks. Windows broke and pieces of glass fell on the speakers' heads. Where did the rocks come from, since all the surrounding streets were paved? And where did the so-called 'dissidents' get their anger from?

The police heard nothing.

The chorus of terrorists turned at one point towards the Police Chief Colonel Kamoutsis, who was watching.

'Chief! Today we're going to get them all!'

'Steady, chaps, steady,' replied the police chief in a soothing voice.

On the third floor, as Lambrakis began his speech about peace and disarmament, shouts were heard:

'Down with peace!'

'We want war!'

'Lambrakis, you're dead.'

At one point, with rocks falling like rain through the windows, Lambrakis interrupted his speech. 'Attention! Attention! This is Deputy Lambrakis speaking. As a representative of the nation and the people, I charge that there is a plot to murder me, and I call upon the Minister of Northern Greece, the Prefect, the Public Prosecutor, General Mitsou of the gendarmes, the City Police Chief, and the Director of Security in Thessaloniki to protect the lives of the friends of peace who are gathered here, and my own life …'

Meanwhile Giorgos Tsarouchas, EDA deputy for Kavala, arrived at the rally, and tried to find the senior police officer. While talking to police, he was hit on the head by thugs. An ambulance arrived and took him to the hospital, but along the way the ambulance was stopped and two or three men started hitting him around the face and head, shouting 'you're going to die'. They had to stop what they were doing – as they were hitting him, their leader said: 'Stop! It's not him!' Eventually Tsarouchas was taken to hospital …

Back at the rally, Lambrakis was finishing his speech with the words of Christ: 'Blessed are the peacemakers, for they shall be called the children of God'. The parastate chorus replied from the sidewalk: 'Down with Peace!', 'We want war!' Once again, the Deputy addressed an appeal: 'Mr Police Chief, Mr Prefect, Mr Public Prosecutor, Mr Minister! This is Deputy Lambrakis speaking to you. You can hear me over the loudspeakers. I hold you responsible. This morning we reported that there is a plot to kill me. And a few moments ago, on my way here, I was assaulted by thugs. As I speak, I have been hurt. Why have you taken no measures? I ask for your protection. And again, I hold you responsible …'

Outside the hall there were 150 uniformed policemen and 50 in plain clothes, headed by General Mitsou, Colonel Kamoutsis, and Security Director Dolkas. The terrorists numbered no more than 60. However, assaults were mounted against two deputies, stones were thrown into the hall in which the rally was being held, there were provocations and an assault on a Red Cross ambulance, for which no one was ever charged …

The motorised gang of assassins – a black motorcycle, two motorbikes, a bicycle with a basket at the back, and Gotzamanis' three-wheeled truck – cleared the Venizelou-Ermou intersection of all vehicles. They would pull up beside cars or pass them, obliging them to leave the space free for the three-wheeler

Gotzamanis parked outside the Cosmopolite. He was approached by a man from the market police with whom he had a ten-minute conversation. Later Gotzamanis turned into Spandoni Street and waited.

Police officers went up to the hall and confirmed that the area was 'cleared' and that people would soon be able to leave.

Lambrakis and the friends of peace gathered together after the rally ended and went down to the entrance. An officer stopped them and told them to wait. 'The area is still being cleared … ' In the street outside the entrance there were two majors, a warrant officer and 15 or so policemen.

Lambrakis saw Colonel Kamoutsis opposite. He crossed over and complained. He asked for protection. The officer at the entrance to the building called Lambrakis and 15 others, no more, to leave. Had more people accompanied them, they might have stopped the crime with their sheer volume.

Traffic had been prohibited. Uniformed gendarmes were standing everywhere in the vicinity and at the intersection of Venizelou and Ermou.

Lambrakis headed toward the Cosmopolite Hotel. When he arrived in front of the Spandoni Street exit, he saw three or four unknown faces coming towards him from Ermou Street with sinister intentions: a pincer movement.

He turned towards the policemen and protested: 'This is a disgrace …' Those were his last words. It was 10:15pm.

On Spandoni Street, somebody pointed him out: 'That's him.'

The sound of a motorcycle revving up was heard 6-8 metres away. Like lightning, the three-wheeler with the covered licence plate raced towards him. He was clubbed on the head and thrown onto the asphalt. Then the vehicle continued on like a shot towards the sea.

'Get him, get him!' shouted many voices. The police did not get him.

A brave man, Manolis Hatziapostolou, jumped into the cart of the three-wheeler. The assassin in the back tried to hide his face so he could not be recognised.

'I jumped on him and grabbed him by the hair but then he took out a revolver. With the jolts of the careening motorcycle, we both fell on the floor of the cart. I kicked him in the face with all my might to save my life. To protect his face from my blows he had to put the pistol down, which fell onto the road outside Loumidis. I shout "Help!"; so does he. We fight. We are outside the offices of the newspaper Ellinikos Vorras. *He soon falls down in the cart, unconscious from my blows. Then I turn my attention to the driver and try to make him stop the motor. I break the glass on the side of the cab. Then he got mad. We stop at the intersection outside the Titania cinema [Ed. note: more than 1km from the scene of the crime]. The driver gets out and jumps on me. He takes a truncheon out of his pocket and hits me twice on the head.*

I feel dizzy and at one point I can see a gang of thugs around me, who are starting to shout

"He's a communist, he killed people".

At the same time though, passers-by are starting to gather around and support me. "The kid's all right," they said, "the other guy was bashing him on the head with a piece of wood." And then I shouted: "I'm a friend of peace!" And people started defending me more resolutely. Many people ran to protect me. Meanwhile the traffic police arrived. They arrested the driver and wanted to take me too. In the beginning I didn't want to go with them. They said "We're not going to hurt you." I said "I'll tell you what we're going to do." So we stood in the middle of the street, where I chose the taxi we'd take. I didn't trust them; they might have brought some thug taxi of their own and dumped me outside of town. I didn't let anyone else in the taxi. I went with one traffic cop to the first aid station and from there they took me to the hospital.'

A pool of blood remained on the asphalt.

Lambrakis was taken to the Ahepa hospital, where he began his battle with Charon [the ferryman of Hades].

All of Greece was holding its breath…

A political upheaval followed. There was a general outcry all over the country from forces of the Left. Giorgos Papandreou, then leader of the opposition, stated:

'The Centre Union party, before the Nation and international public opinion, accuses the leader of ERE, Mr. Karamanlis, as the instigator of the political assassination of Deputy Grigoris Lambrakis' (*Thessaloniki* newspaper, 24.5.1963).

Avgi wrote: 'But haven't the foreign puppets been sated with blood. Haven't they had enough of ruination and grief? Hasn't Greece been sufficiently humiliated? Just a month earlier people deplored their barbarity, but still they insist on this shameful policy, because they have no other.'

Grigoris Lambrakis fought death for one hundred hours in room 155 of the Ahepa hospital. The 'great oak' died on 27 May 1963 at 1:22am, but the slogan 'Lambrakis Lives' rang out immediately throughout all of Greece and rapidly spread across its borders.

IV
The outcry amongst the Greek people

'In the person of Grigoris Lambrakis, the worthy son of Greece, certain people sought to murder peace, bravery and humanity. But can the sun ever be killed? All of Greece is on its feet. Not for a burial, but for a resurrection.'

Dido Sotiriou

The Greek people, in a state of shock, began to express their feelings in Thessaloniki, honouring the great man who had died, and wrath against his assassins. 'The great death brought the explosion.'

On Monday 27 May 1963, the body of Lambrakis was brought by rail to Athens. Giorgos Maniatis recollects the scene at Larissa Station:

'There are a few thousand of us. Some of us were beaten yesterday and the day before yesterday. Our eyes are black from punches. But they are also black for another reason. The time is eleven. Five minutes to twelve. Four minutes to twelve. The train arrives. A special train. The engine and freight car ZΠT 6.148 are bringing us the deceased from Thessaloniki. They remove the body. Resting on him is the flag of Greece.'

The body of Lambrakis was laid out in the chapel of the Orthodox Cathedral for people to pay their respects. Tuesday 28 May was the day of the funeral and all roads led to the Cathedral. The people declared their resounding presence on the last journey of the Marathon runner of peace, from the Cathedral to the First Cemetery.

Honour guard beside Lambrakis' coffin:
Manos Katrakis, Daphne Skoura and Mitsos Lygizos

Giorgos Maniatis recorded the following exchange in *Roads of Peace*:

'"Wasn't it like this at Palamas's funeral as well?" asked an old-timer.
  "Are you kidding? It wasn't like this even when the Occupation ended!"
  Sidewalks, construction sites, piles of rubble and the high ground in front of the cemetery were all full of people. We approach. We arrive at the entrance to the Cemetery. The body is behind glass and the carriage stops. The motor is turned off. The people touch it. They push it, they lift it. They bring it forward. From a

construction site, a voice rings out: "Every young person is Lambrakis". And the people take the phrase and promise: "Ev-ery young per-son is Lam-bra-kis!"

That Marathon funeral was a grief-stricken outcry against organised crime and the spectre of fascism by the hundreds of thousands of people who had poured onto the streets, into the squares, onto their balconies, with sorrow in their eyes and red carnations in their hands, as well as a candle for the world tomorrow. Among these thousands, one could distinguish the heads of visitors from abroad who had come to walk behind the great man's body: the representative of the Italian Senate, Mr. Secchia, the Italian MPs Sardini and Luzzato, the British MP Malcolm Macmillan, the Cypriot MP from AKEL Andreas Ziartidis, representatives of Lord Russell and Canon Collins, Professor B. Steiner, vice-president of the International Federation of Resistance Fighters, Abbot Ronio and Charles Bossy from the French Peace Movement, Z. Husek, President of the Federation of National Resistance Fighters of Czechoslovakia, and other British and French people, journalists, tourists, and fraternal spirits from other countries.'

Artist M. Argyrakis depicts the assassination of Lambrakis

V
Grief in the cultural world

Among the first to be at Lambrakis' side as he lay dying in the Ahepa hosital on 23 May were Yannis Imvriotis, Yannis Ritsos and Mikis Theodorakis, who issued the following joint statement:

'A short while ago we watched Lambrakis struggling with death. A team of assassins decided to kill him in cold blood and a despicable criminal executed the order with brutal indifference. The fascist monster shed blood on the streets of Thessaloniki. Let us look calmly for whoever is hiding behind the assassins and let us all stand loyal to the Greek people, who are being murdered to force others into submission.

Scholars, workers, artists, if each one of us just does our duty, then there is hope that we will be able to root out the criminals. Then there is hope that the blood shed in Thessaloniki will choke the vile assassins forever.'

The assassination of Lambrakis shattered Greece's cultural world. Yannis Ritsos and Nikiforos Vrettakos both wrote funeral epigrams for the hero of peace, after his death was announced on 27 May. Yannis Ritsos wrote:

The great oak fell to earth in a huge struggle.
Birds and leaves came to a standstill in the sky
while Greece held him in her lap

on a deep purple evening in May.
And while rage causes her pores to sweat blood
it explodes among the blessed people
and raises him up, high, as a messianic beam,
supporting the dome in the temple of peace.

In his epigram, Nikiforos Vrettakos wrote:

Raising on his shoulders the trophy of Marathon,
the handsome man descends into Hades, dead,

where the eternal Greeks await him. He brings but
half the message: 'WE HAVE …
Behind me, others bring you the rest: WE HAVE TRIUMPHED.
I wasn't meant to arrive so soon
in the land of Plataia and in Marathon
the Persians killed me.'

'Lament of a Nation', a poem by Victoria Theodorou, was published in *Epitheorisi Technis* (Art Review) in May 1963:

I came to sit on the stairs of the black door
like a tombstone, where you were closed and lifeless,
to voice my pain and malediction.
Ah, one by one the most worthy are leaving!
Heaven's stars lie extinguished in the dust.
I give you my hair which for three nights
I washed with the rainwater of May
that you might turn your storm-tossed head.
Gazelle, you bested wild creatures in your leap
But Charon was faster than you
and myriad lives he unwittingly gave you
for which he now berates himself, with bitter regret.

In the same issue of *Epitheorisi Technis*, the lead article entitled 'Conscience Alert!' was dedicated to the assassination of Lambrakis. It said:

'The heinous fascist crime, the assassination of the Deputy, scientist and athlete Grigoris Lambrakis, has shaken all hearts in our country like an earthquake. It was a conscience alert, to a degree unprecedented in recent times and manifested everywhere.

The pain over the murdered hero was felt across the nation, as was indignation and rage, and the decision was made nationwide to find and break the criminal arm. To break it before the country is plunged into the abyss of medieval fascism. And to restore the temple of democracy to its first cradle.'

But the torch of peace did not fall from the hands of the murdered Marathon marcher, nor was it extinguished by the bloodshed, as the executioners had hoped. It was immediately taken up by an entire nation to become a banner of victory and a sword of struggle. And in this nationwide struggle, the men and women of the pen, the brush, the chisel, and of discourse, all people of culture, were the first to declare their presence. And they showed, once again, a unanimity and generosity of soul worthy of their great traditions. First at his deathbed they listened, with bated breath, to the final beats of his heart, and were the first to protest, first in the torrent of people who accompanied this fearless man on the road to the pantheon of heroes, first in the decision to fight, first everywhere, all together, irrespective of any differences in their ideas and convictions, alongside the people – leaders and soldiers simultaneously.

They gave life, flesh and bones to the words of Isocrates: 'And they addressed those leaders'. At this critical moment, the people of culture showed themselves worthy leaders of the nation.

The Society of Greek Authors, the Actors' Guild and Art Group A addressed an appeal to cultural and artistic organisations and periodicals. The appeal was co-signed by the *Tomi* (*Turning Point*) Artists' Society and by Pelos Katselis, president of the Theatre Art Directors. Below are excerpts from their appeal:

'The attack against Grigoris Lambrakis is not simply the murder of a representative of the nation, a university teacher and an athlete of democracy. It is an action directed against democracy itself, against freedom and thought, and establishes murder as a means of imposing political ideas. It has been thus assessed by all thinking Greeks both at home and abroad as a victory for the law of the jungle. In confronting this crime, which augurs profound abnormalities and the total abolition of democracy and freedom, Greeks of culture and the arts have become aware of its significance and in consideration of their great responsibility, feel the profound obligation to alert our consciences.'

A few months after the assassination, Kostas Porphyris published a book entitled *Lambrakis the Fearless Warrior.*

VI
Lambrakis Democratic Youth (LDY)

The popular uprising over the assassination of Lambrakis sparked one of history's great democratic regeneration movements, particularly among young people. The main expression of this was the Lambrakis Democratic Youth, a movement that functioned as a catalyst in the defeat of the right-wing National Radical Union party (ERE) in the elections of November 1963. On 9 July 1963, the founding Declaration of the Lambrakis Democratic Youth was published and signed by 30 people.

The LDY was also a major cultural movement. For example, in 1964, Mikis Theodorakis announced at a press conference the launch of a nationwide cultural campaign to combat illiteracy, to establish a University of the People, to clean up

25 Μάη 1963
ἡ ἐφημερίδα «ΘΕΣΣΑΛΟΝΙΚΗ» δημοσιεύει τὴν προ-
κήρυξη ποὺ κυκλοφόρησε στὴ Θεσσαλονίκη...

ΓΡΗΓΟΡΗΣ ΛΑΜΠΡΑΚΗΣ

Β ο υ λ ε υ τ ὴ ς
- Βαλκανιονίκης · Πρωταθλητὴς τοῦ ἅλμα-
τος εἰς μῆκος
- Ὑφηγητὴς τοῦ Πανεπιστημίου Ἀθηνῶν
- Ὀδοιπόρος τοῦ Ὀλντερμάστον
- Μαραθωνοδρόμος τῆς Εἰρήνης
Ο ΓΡΗΓΟΡΙΟΣ ΛΑΜΠΡΑΚΗΣ

Νὰ πιὸ εἶναι τὸ πρόσφατο θύμα τῆς δολο-
φονικῆς ἐπίδεσης τῶν νεοφασιστῶν τῆς
Ε.Ρ.Ε. ποὺ τοὺς ὀργανώνει ἡ κυβέρνηση
τῆς βίας.
- Νὰ διαλυδοῦν οἱ νεοφασιστικὲς ὀργανώ-
σεις
- Νὰ φύγει ἡ κυβέρνηση τοῦ αἵματος
- Δὲν θὰ περάσει ὁ Φασισμὸς
- Ἡ Δημοκρατία καὶ ἡ Ἑλλάδα θὰ ζήσουν
Ε.Δ.Α. Θεσσαλονίκης

• Βουλευτὴς
Πειραιῶς
('Ανεξάρτητος)

• Ὑφηγητὴς
Ἰατρικῆς
Πανεπιστημίου
Ἀθηνῶν

• Ἀντιπρόεδρος
Ἑλληνικῆς
Ἐπιτροπῆς
γιὰ τὴν
Διεθνῆ "Ὑφεση
καὶ Εἰρήνη

• Πολυνίκης
Βαλκανικῶν
Ἀγώνων

• Μαραθωνοδρόμος
τῆς Εἰρήνης

ΔΟΛΟΦΟΝΗΘΗΚΕ...

ἀπὸ τοὺς νεοφασίστες, ποὺ ὀργανώνει ἡ Κυβέρνηση
Τὸ πολιτικὸ ἔγκλημα ἀνοίγει τὸ δρόμο στὸ Φασισμο
Α Π Α Ι Τ Ε Ι Σ Τ Ε
• Να τιμωρηθοῦν οἱ δολοφόνοι
• Νὰ διαλυθοῦν οἱ νεοφασιστικὲς ὀργανώσεις
• Νὰ φύγει ἡ Κυβέρνηση του αἵματος

and popularise sport, to create cultural societies in every village and neighbourhood, and to establish an annual Greek Youth Festival (*Roads of Peace,* January 1964).

VII
International reaction

The assassination of Grigoris Lambrakis, famous participant in the Aldermaston and Marathon marches, naturally sparked a great international protest movement. In London, Pat Potttle, who had taken part in the first Marathon Peace March representing Bertrand Russell, read Russell's message on the occasion of the murder to a large meeting. A demonstration brightened the dark streets of London with the slogans 'Lambrakis was murdered because he was fighting for disarmament', 'The Greek Peace Hero – first victim of Polaris missiles in Greece', 'Amnesty? For Democracy to shine', 'The Greek Government rules with gangs of assassins'.

According to Michael Randle,

'The murder of Lambrakis had a huge impact on Committee of 100 and Campaign for Nuclear Disarmament people – and indeed on the Left generally – in this country and you could see graffiti in many parts of London condemning the murder. A reporter from the CND journal *Sanity*, David Bolton, attended the funeral in Athens, which turned into a gigantic march for peace and freedom. Bolton described it in his report as the greatest march he had ever seen.'

Protest march in London

Meanwhile, the Greek Embassy was inundated with telegrams of protest: 22 Labour Party MPs; the Committee of 100; Cypriots in London; organisations of Jews against Nazism, and trade unions – they all besieged the Greek Embassy with protests and messages, which the embassy returned as unacceptable. The Karamanlis government did the same. And the Labour Party noted: 'Even Franco and Salazar don't return the protests sent by British citizens …'

The demonstration outside the Greek embassy in London was repeated every evening for an entire week. Demonstrations, protests and articles in the press made the rounds of Europe, then crossed oceans and continents.

In Genoa, 4,000 protesters shouted 'Murderers!'; 'Democracy for Greece!'. In Rome the protesters were holding photographs of Lambrakis and banners on which was written: 'Lambrakis, like Matteotti' (an Italian MP who, in 1924, was murdered by fascists after exposing their electoral fraud), 'Assassins' and 'Stop fascism'. In the Soviet Union a large protest meeting was held. The speakers were M. Kotov, Secretary of the Soviet Committee for the Defence of Peace, Boris Polevoy and Stella Petrou, a Greek-Cypriot student at Lumumba University.

In Cyprus, all the newspapers, the most significant representatives of culture, AKEL (the communist party), and people at rallies in the workplace issued protest resolutions. In Czechoslovakia, the radio station and newspapers expressed the people's anger. From Israel, the MAPAM party sent a protest telegram. The Polish Peace Committee, the Union of Polish Students, the Medical Academy of Warsaw, the Association of Resistance Fighters, Polish MPs,

The Lambrakis medal established by the Greek Peace Committee EEDYE

newspapers and radio stations all protested. German newspapers excoriated the crime and the portent of fascism in Greece. Reactions from France, Denmark, Bulgaria and many other countries were much the same.

Large organisations such as the World Federation of Democratic Youth, the General Confederation of Labour of Italy, the World Federation of Trade Unions, the Executive Council of British Coalminers, 85 Italian senators, Jacques Duclos, and Italian intellectuals all expressed their horror at the heinous murder and joined their voices to block the road to making crime the law.

In honour of Lambrakis, the World Peace Council, at its first session after the assassination, created a Lambrakis Medal to be awarded in recognition of exceptional services to the struggle for peace. It is a silver medal portraying his face in relief with his name on one side and the dove of Picasso with the words 'World Peace Council' on the other.

EEDYE also established a Lambrakis Medal, which was awarded after the dictatorship to Nelson Mandela and to the Greek peace activists Yannis Ritsos, Nikiforos Vrettakos, Dido Sotiriou, Stavros Kanellopoulos, Aleka Katseli, Aspasia Papathanasiou, Tassos Engolfopoulos, Vagelis Hatziangeli (Chania), Apostolos Apostolou (Mytilene), Christodoulos Mavrovitis (Thessaloniki), and Vassilis Georgakopoulos (trade unionist).

In 1985, the Lambrakis medal was awarded to the Committee of Mothers, Wives and Relatives of activists who had been murdered or imprisoned or had disappeared in El Salvador.

VIII
The prosecution

The prosecution in the mid-1960s of those responsible for Lambrakis' murder evolved into a major political, legal and journalistic battle. Giannis Voultepsis (*Avgi*), G. Bertsos (*Eleftheria*) and Giorgos Romaios (*Ta Nea*) were leading figures in the journalistic investigation. In the court, the courageous figure of Christos Sartzetakis stood out, a jurist of high integrity who was called upon to investigate the Deputy's death, and uncovered the police conspiracy to murder him. He indicted many high-ranking officers who were later reinstated by the junta, under whose rule Sartzetakis was imprisoned. When democracy was restored, he was released, became a supreme justice of the Court of Cassation, and was elected President of the Hellenic Republic in 1985.

The assassination of Lambrakis was a strong omen pointing to the junta four years later. The same machinery that murdered Lambrakis played a major role in the *coup d'état* of 21 April 1967 and in the seven years of subsequent tyranny against the Greek people, that culminated in the betrayal of Cyprus.

After the dictatorship, author and former Prime Minister Panagiotis Kanellopoulos wrote: 'The group of officers that imposed the coup in April 1967 may even have had a hand in the episodes that, on 22 May 1963, led to the mortal injury of Deputy Grigoris Lambrakis.' (*Essays in History: How we arrived at 21 April 1967*)

IX
The institution of the Marathon Marches

After the assassination of Lambrakis, Marathon Marches were held every year until the coup in 1967, and many more were held after the fall of the junta in 1974, initially organised by AKE, then by EEDYE and later jointly, and in the post-cold-war era by EEDYE alone.

What the pre-dictatorship Marathon Marches signified can be seen from the description of the Second Marathon Peace March on 17 May 1964 by Takis Benas (Secretary of EDA Youth from 1960-1963 and of Lambrakis Democratic Youth from 1963-1967):

Takis Benas

'Many preliminary events were held all over Greece, in neighbourhoods, in cities, there were hundreds if not thousands of discussions and meetings on the local and sectoral level. There wasn't a single sector, district, school, university, factory, or indeed any unit of life that hadn't planned its participation with its own Marathon March committee. In this way, a spirit of rivalry was created. Every group wanted its participation to be an event: an event for Kaisariani, for Kokkinia, for Peristeri, etc. And it wasn't only rivalry over who would have the largest block of people walking in the march, but also rivalry over the events planned as part of the march as well: intellectual, theatrical, musical, and poetic events.

In essence, the march didn't start at 6:00 in the morning, but the previous evening, when a kind of overnight fair was set up in Nea Makri with tents for people to sleep in. There must have been a couple of thousand people taking part. All night there was singing, plays were performed, etc. People slept for a few hours and in the morning they were the first to reach the Mound. To bring all these people to the Mound, coaches were used, the famous "peace coaches". Every neighbourhood, every sector, every factory rented a coach – which actually created a traffic problem.

The Second Marathon Peace March[1] was highly successful in terms of both mass participation and the cultural events that were held at the various stops along the way: in Nea Makri, Harvati and up to Ayia Paraskevi, which was the last stop. The march took place, as we used to say then, in "bunches". One bunch consisted of people from Piraeus, another of trade unionists, or students, or people from a particular province,

Members of Lambrakis Democratic Youth headed by Mikis Theodorakis

and so on. Each bunch had its own leadership, programme, internal events and organisation (e.g. what they would eat for lunch, etc.) Everybody brought their own guitars ... So the route wasn't a plain march or ordinary walk, it was a big party.'

Marathon peace marches were also held in 1965 (the third) and 1966 (the fourth). The fifth, which had been planned for 1967, was cancelled when the dictatorship was imposed on 21 April that year.

Among the messages that had already been sent from abroad for the march that did not take place, the message from Bertrand Russell, then 95 years old, was prophetic. He wrote:

'... The March has come to symbolise the desire on the part of the Greek citizens to live in a country no longer dominated by a military clique and a corrupt monarchy ... Not since the death of the great Greek hero, Gregory Lambrakis, has the Marathon to Athens March assumed such momentous significance as it has this year.

The United States is waging a war of criminal barbarity against the people of Vietnam. It is using every kind of experimental weapon against the Vietnamese people, because the people of Vietnam have dared to struggle for a better way of life, for social justice, and for an end to exploitation and for true national independence. Every one of these goals, for which the Vietnamese sacrificed so much, is as relevant to the situation in Greece today. The United States has used toxic chemicals, poison gas, jelly-gasoline napalm, white phosphorus and fragmentation bombs.

The United States has bombed hospitals, schools, sanitoria, leprosoria, pagodas and churches. These acts compare with the atrocities committed by the Nazis against the people of Greece in the last war... Let the march begin the bitter struggle for a new Greece, a Greece without poverty, a Greece without police terror, a Greece without military dictatorship, a Greece with genuine democracy and full social justice. As in the days of Lambrakis, I send my heartfelt greetings and feelings of solidarity to the people of Greece on the great occasion of the historic Fifth Marathon to Athens March. I urge all Greeks to express their support for our International War Crimes Tribunal, because our Tribunal is seeking to investigate the crimes committed against the people of Vietnam, crimes which the people of Greece know through their own experience. Our War Crimes Tribunal speaks for the conscience of all who oppose American brutality in Vietnam and dictatorship in Greece and we rely on the people of Greece for their full support.'

The message was signed and dated 12 April 1967, just nine days before the junta of the colonels was imposed.

X
Monuments to Lambrakis

To honour Lambrakis, efforts were made immediately after his death to erect monuments in his memory. It started at his grave in the First Cemetery of Athens, where a monument created by the sculptor Ch. Daradimos was placed. In 1989, a statue of Lambrakis was erected on the route from Marathon to Athens specifically in Pallini, after collaboration between the Community of Pallini and EEDYE. The cost was covered by the activist Despina Pouli through the Community of Pallini. A Lambrakis monument was likewise placed on the site where he was mortally injured in Thessaloniki, on the initiative of the Municipality; it was unveiled on 22 May 1988.

Many efforts were made to preserve the Lambrakis house in Kerasitsa and to make it a Peace Museum. The house was declared a heritage building in 1989, when the Minister of Culture was Giorgos Mylonas and the General Secretary of the Ministry was Makis Trikoukis. According to the ministerial decision, the house was designated a heritage site because 'it was the family home of Grigoris Lambrakis, a distinguished physician, significant athlete with Balkan victories that brought honour to Greece, and an important peace

Pallini: Lambrakis' sons, Giorgos (left) and Grigoris (right) with Despina Pouli

activist, one of the protagonists of the peace movement in Greece.' In the end, the house was demolished, despite the efforts of Grigoris' cousin, Odysseas Tsoukopoulos, to prevent it.

And finally, the Municipality of Tegea placed a statue of Lambrakis in Kerasitsa, in the Square named after him on the road to Sparta. The statue was unveiled by the President of the Hellenic Republic, Karolos Papoulias, on 9 June 2007.

Footnote

1. The organising committee of the Second Marathon March comprised the following: Melis Nikolaidis, Gen. Sec. of the Society of Greek Authors, Aleka Katseli, Fotis Kontoglou, Orestis Kanellis, Vassilis Mesolongitis, Andreas Barkoulis and Giorgos Sikeliotis. From the student movement there were: Apostolos Besis (vice President of EFEE (National Student Union of Greece), Giannis Giannoulopoulos (Gen.Sec. of EFEE), Vias Leivadas, Al. Kalofolias, K. Vardakis, A. Manolakos, M. Mylonakis (head of Panspoudastiki [another university students' union]), Th. Tsouknidas.

APPENDIX

Peace Movement Chronicle
1945-2000

Struggles for peace have a history as long as wars, which number more than 5,000 over the past five millennia, the most destructive being the two world wars of the 20th century. It is thus natural that the sufferings inflicted by war are accompanied by the pursuit of peace in human societies. This is registered above all in global literature, the most characteristic examples being the ancient Greek tragedies, but also seen in institutions from antiquity that survive in one form or another today, such as the Olympic Games and the Delphic Amphiktyons.

The development of the peace movement as a mass popular action is closely linked with the growth of the labour movement in the 19th century. Marx and Engels associated a state of permanent peace with the abolition of exploitative capitalist relations, pointing out that, in a socialist world peace should be the international rule because the national leader will always be the same: Labour.

Many peace organisations have come into being since then. In 1892, the first permanent international organisation was established: the International Peace Bureau (IPB), which is based in Geneva, and was awarded the Nobel Prize for Peace in 1910.

In Greece, the peace movement developed to some degree during the First World War and the Asia Minor expedition, but much more during the 1930s. The Panhellenic Anti-War-Anti-Fascist Congress took place in Athens on 3-4 June 1934, on the intiative of Nikos Karvounis, Dimitris Glinos and other intellectuals as well as officials of the labour movement.

After World War Two, the peace movement took on massive global dimensions and many different forms, as revealed by this chronicle.

* * *

1945

8 May: The war in Europe ended with the occupation of the Reichstag by Soviet troops and the surrender of Germany. The following day, 9 May, became the Day of Anti-fascist Victory. Japan continues fighting.

6 August: the US Air Force dropped the first atomic bomb, transforming Hiroshima into a hell and a giant graveyard. Three days later, Nagasaki was also bombed. The new weapons created great concern and fear. Japan surrendered three weeks later, ending World War Two.

24 October: The crowning of the anti-fascist victory was the establishment of the United Nations, with 51 member states initially, the main goal being 'to save the generations to come from the scourge of war' according to its Founding Charter.

1946

Albert Einstein, together with top US scientists, established the Emergency Committee of Atomic Scientists.

1947

12 March: The Truman Doctrine was announced.

15 August: Independence of India and Pakistan

29 November: The UN General Assembly adopted a resolution calling for the partition of Palestine into Jewish and Arab States, with Jerusalem as an international city.

1948

6 August: Wrocław, Poland. A World Conference of Intellectuals for Peace was held, precisely three years after the holocaust of Hiroshima.

24 June: Berlin Blockade imposed by the USSR, the first major post-war crisis.

1949

20-22 April: A World Peace Conference was held simultaneously in Paris and Warsaw. The Cold War prevented the delegates from gathering in the same city. The conference concluded by establishing the World Peace Council (WPC).

1950

15 March: By decision of the Stockholm Conference, the WPC circulated the Stockholm Appeal for a ban on nuclear weapons.

11 November: The Nobel Prize for Literature was awarded to Bertrand Russell.

1951

5 March: The 22-year-old peace activist Nikos Nikiforidis was executed in Thessaloniki. He was condemned to death by an extraordinary court martial for gathering signatures to the Stockholm Appeal for Peace.

1952

18 February: Greece became a member of NATO.

Nelson Mandela organises a civil disobedience campaign against apartheid laws in South Africa.

1953

12 October: Agreement signed to establish US bases in Greece.

1954

1 March: The first US hydrogen bomb is tested on the Bikini Atoll in the Pacific Ocean.

1955

The civil rights movement is launched in the US by Rev. Martin Luther King.

18 April: Albert Einstein dies.

15 May: A Declaration is published, signed by 77 public figures, for the founding of the Greek Committee for International Détente and Peace (EEDYE).

9 July: The Russell-Einstein Manifesto is published in London.

1956

26 July: Nationalisation of the Suez Canal by Nasser. Unsuccessful intervention by France, Britain and Israel.

23 October: Uprising in Hungary

1957

In the Canadian village of Pugwash, Nova Scotia, the Pugwash Movement of scientists and scholars for peace is established.

4 October: The launch of Sputnik I, the first satellite in space, marks the beginning of the space age.

1958

First March from London to Aldermaston in favour of nuclear disarmament. It was turned round the next year, starting from Aldermaston to London.

9 May: The first issue of the magazine *Roads of Peace* is published in Greece.

1959

January 1: Cuban Revolution led by Fidel Castro and Che Guevara overthrows the Batista dictatorship.

1960

1 August: Cyprus becomes an independent republic.

1961

2 October: Appeal launched by EEDYE 'To the political world and public opinion'. Among those present was the British classical scholar, author and Marxist, George Thomson.

1962

7-14 July: World Peace Congress in Moscow.

13-28 October: Cuban missile crisis. The USA and USSR hover on the brink of nuclear war. Interventions by Bertrand Russell with messages to Kennedy and Khrushchev in favour of a peaceful solution.

23-24 November: Visit of Bishop Makarios to Ankara.

1963

Early January: The Bertrand Russell Youth League for Nuclear Disarmament is established in Athens.

12-14 April: Peace March from Aldermaston to London in which a delegation from EEDYE takes part, with Grigoris Lambrakis, Manolis Glezos, Leonidas Kyrkos, Betty Ambatielou and Spyros Linardatos.

21 April: The First Marathon Peace March takes place in Greece despite being banned by the Karamanlis government.

22 May: Grigoris Lambrakis is assassinated in Thessaloniki by the fascist parastate.

16 August: Demonstration of young people from the peace movement to celebrate the agreement on a partial nuclear test ban between the USA and USSR in Moscow.

28 August: March on Washington by 200,000 US citizens that ended at the Lincoln Memorial where Martin Luther King made his historic 'I have a dream' speech.

29 September: Establishment of Bertrand Russell Peace Foundation announced in London.

22 November: John F. Kennedy, President of the United States, assassinated in Dallas, Texas.

1964

17 May: The second Peace March from Marathon to Athens is held with massive public participation.

5-9 July: International Conference in Algiers on the denuclearisation of the Mediterranean. Participation of EEDYE

The Nobel Peace Prize is awarded to Martin Luther King.

Nelson Mandela is sentenced to life imprisonment for his anti-apartheid activities.

1965

July: The Centre Union government in Greece is toppled by a Palace coup. Many demonstrations and protests take place.

21 July: Assassination of Sotiris Petroulas.

1967

21 April: Imposition of military dictatorship in Athens. All peace organisations are banned, and thousands of their members are arrested and exiled.

6 June: Launching of the Six-Day War in the Middle East.

9 October: Assassination of Che Guevara in Bolivia.

1968

4 April: Assassination of Martin Luther King in Memphis Tennessee.

14 May: Strike movement begins in France, fuels broader youth uprising and

precipitates the events of the 1968 French May.

20 August: The Warsaw Pact invades Czechoslovakia to crush the Prague spring.

1969

20 July: The first man to walk on the moon: the Apollo 11 mission.

15 August: Woodstock Festival. Three days of music and peace. 400,000 people attend.

Willy Brandt elected chancellor of West Germany and inaugurates the policy of détente with the USSR.

1970s

The 1970s have been described as the decade of détente and indeed many events and developments changed the international political climate for the better. Among them were the Helsinki Conference on Security and Co-operation in Europe (1.8.1975), and the historic victory of the Vietnamese people over the US and the end of the war in Indochina. In addition, the 'Carnation Revolution' in Portugal dealt one of the final blows to colonialism.

1970

4 September: Salvador Allende is elected president of Chile and proclaims a peaceful road to socialism.

1972

21 February: US President Richard Nixon visits China. Ping-pong diplomacy bears fruit.

1973

11 September: Fascist coup in Chile by Augusto Pinochet who topples the democratically elected government of Salvador Allende.

1974

15 July: Coup ousts Makarios as president of Cyprus. Within days the Turkish army invades the island and, soon after, the junta in Athens falls.

1975

30 April: Fall of Saigon to North Vietnamese. Reunification of Vietnam begins.

1 August: The Helsinki Final Act on Principles Guiding Relations between Participating States is signed by 33 countries of Europe, Canada and the US.

1976

29-31 October: World Conference of Solidarity with the People of Cyprus in Frankfurt.

1977

EEDYE reissues the magazine *Roads of Peace*, publisher Dinos Tsiros, editor Alexis Karrer.

1978

9-12 February: International Conference on Peace in the Mediterranean

13 May-1 July: First UN Special Session on Disarmament

1979

18 June: Signing of the Strategic Arms Limitation Treaty (SALT) II agreement by Jimmy Carter and Leonid Brezhnev in Vienna.

NATO decides to deploy 572 medium-range Pershing and Cruise missiles in Europe, while the USSR decides to deploy nuclear-armed SS20s. In the Federal Republic of Germany, the Krefeld Appeal against the euro-missiles circulates.

1980s

'The Most Dangerous Decade', according to Ken Coates, one of the founders, leaders and moving forces of European Nuclear Disarmament (END), which saw an unprecedented upsurge of the European and global movement for peace and nuclear disarmament. In 1980, the International Physicians for the Prevention of Nuclear War (IPPNW) was established, with co-presidents, an American and a Soviet physician, Bernard Lown and Evgeny Chazov respectively. IPPNW organised scientific research into the devastating effects on health and the environment, declaring that 'there is no cure for nuclear war, just prevention'. IPPNW was awarded the Nobel Peace Prize in 1985.

23-27 September: The World Parliament of the Peoples for Peace is held in Sofia.

Manchester, England is the first city to declare itself a 'nuclear-free zone' by decision of its City Council.

1981

In 1981, the movement 'Generals for Peace and Disarmament' was created, with the participation of retired NATO generals and admirals. Representing Greece were General (ret.) Giorgos Koumanakos and Admiral (ret.) Miltiadis Papathanasiou. Among the members of the Movement were the German Major General Gert Bastian, who took an active part in the Green Movement in the Federal Republic of Germany, Italian General Nino Pasti, and French Admiral Antoine Sanguinetti.

22 June-6 August: International Peace March from Copenhagen to Paris for a Nuclear-Weapon-Free Europe.

1982

7 June-9 July: The 2nd Special Session on Disarmament of the United Nations in New York.

12 June: Rally of a million Americans in Central Park, New York on the occasion of the UN Special Session.

2-4 July: First END (European Nuclear Disarmament) Convention in Brussels.

29 July-6 August: International Peace March starting in Stockholm and ending in Vienna.

1983

9-14 May: END Convention in Berlin

22 May: events in Greece to commemorate the 20th anniversary of the assassination of Grigoris Lambrakis.

21-25 June: 'The World Conference against Nuclear War, for Peace, Life and Civilisation' meets in Prague.

5 August 1983: To commemorate the anniversary of Hiroshima, the Acropolis is encircled with the slogan 'Save the Acropolis, peace, life and culture from nuclear disaster'. It is followed by the establishment of the movement 'Acropolis Appeal'. Its president is Rector of the University of Athens, Michalis Stathopoulos.

1984

16 January: The first ever official inter-Balkan conference of experts is held on the theme of a missile-free Balkans.

22 May: Announcement of the 'Initiative of the Six' for nuclear disarmament. Participants are Indira Gandhi, Prime Minister of India; Raul Alfonsin, President of Argentina, Miguel de la Madrid, President of Mexico, Julius Nyrere, President of Tanzania, Olof Palme, Prime Minister of Sweden, and Andreas Papandreou, Prime Minister of Greece.

17-21 July: 3rd European Nuclear Disarmanent Convention in Perugia, Italy. Joint delegation to the meeting of the three Greek peace committees: AKE, EEDYE and KEADEA.

7 September: establishment of the Greek Affiliate of IPPNW.

1985

9-19 May: Events held to celebrate the 40th anniversary of the Anti-fascist Victory of World War Two.

3-5 June: International Peace Conference in Peking (Beijing) organised by the Chinese Association for International Understanding. This was the first peace conference in China for many decades.

1986

15 January: Programme for zero nuclear weapons by 2000 submitted by the President of the USSR, Mikhail Gorbachev.

2 February: United Nations International Year of Peace. Upon a proposal of EEDYE, it is inaugurated in Delphi.

28 February: Swedish Prime Minister Olof Palme assassinated.

28 April: Nuclear disaster at Chernobyl in the Ukraine. Events and discussions are held to abolish even the 'peaceful use' of nuclear energy.

12-15 September: Conference in Kolymbari Chania, Crete, of the International Peace Bureau, on the initiative of AKE and the Cape of Peace, dedicated to Olof Palme. Participants include the UN, many international organisations, and representatives of the Greek peace movement.

15-19 October: World Conference on the International Year of Peace in Copenhagen.

1987

The demand to ban nuclear testing dominates the early months of 1987, on the occasion of the unilateral Soviet moratorium.

17 February: Upon a proposal by the three Greek peace movements, a peace resolution is unanimously adopted by the Parliament of the Hellenes for the first time in its history.

1-5 September: UNESCO conference in Malta. Proposal by Alkis Argyriadis to establish the Right to Peace.

18 September: An agreement is signed by the US and USSR to abolish the Euro-missiles.

1988

20 July: New breach in the Cold War. Agreement on official relations between the EEC and COMECON.

1989

April: Historic meeting in Prague of political parties from the Greek and Turkish communities of Cyprus.

21-22 April: Greek-Turkish conference of movements in Athens regarding a 10% mutual reduction of military expenditure and weapons by both countries.

9 November: Fall of the Berlin Wall. Beginning of German reunification and of the end of the Cold War

The Last Decade of the 20ᵗʰ Century

The collapse of 'existing socialism' in 1989, and the subsequent dissolution of the USSR in 1991, changed the global balance radically. The end of 'Perestroika' also meant the end of the peace spring that had started with unprecedented initiatives in the 1980s, the signing of the Intermediate Nuclear Forces (INF) Treaty and the elimination of the euro-missiles, the launching of the Strategic Arms Reduction Treaties (START) process, and the peaceful resolution of many regional conflicts. A new Europe looked feasible, as proclaimed by the Charter for a New Europe signed in Paris in 1990.

However, the hopes for a new era of peace and disarmament were not realized. The last decade of the 20th century started with two very negative developments; the Gulf War and the dissolution of Yugoslavia. The Gulf War ended with the proclamation of the so-called New World Order by US President George Bush; the dissolution of Yugoslavia in 1991 precipitated bloody wars on its territory culminating in NATO's war on Serbia in 1999, the first war on European soil since World War Two.

Yet, there were also some positive steps such as the Earth Summit in Rio in 1992, the Chemical Weapons Convention (CWC) in 1993, the election of Nelson Mandela as President of South Africa in 1994, the World Social Summit in Copenhagen in 1995, the signing of the Comprehensive Nuclear-Test-Ban Treaty (CTBT) in 1996, and of the Ottawa Mine Ban Treaty in 1997.

All these achievements became possible with the emergence of an International Civil Society, which gave birth to the new social movements of the 21st century, the World Social Forum, the European Social Forum, and so on.

In this way, the vision of a new peaceful Europe in a new and peaceful world retains its dynamism.

TO ENTER
THE 21 ST CENTURY
WITHOUT
NUCLEAR WEAPONS

New Soviet peace proposals
outlined by Mikhail Gorbachev,
General Secretary of the
CPSU Central Committee,
in his Statement of January 15, 1986

«ΠΛΟΙΟ ΤΗΣ ΕΙΡΗΝΗΣ»

Ο γύρος της Γης σε 86 μέρες

(2 Νοεμβρίου 1990 - 27 Ιανουαρίου 1991)

Πέμπτη 1 Νοεμβρίου ΟΛΥΜΠΙΑ: 11 π.μ. Εναρξη Ειρηνοδρομίας

                                              4-6 μ.μ. Εκδήλωση αναχώρησης

Παρασκευή 2 Νοεμβρίου ΠΕΙΡΑΙΑ:
    (ακτή ΞΑΒΕΡΗ)   5.30 μ.μ. Αφιξη φλόγας από Ολυμπία

ΕΛΛΗΝΙΚΗ ΕΠΙΤΡΟΠΗ ΥΠΟΔΟΧΗΣ
c/o «Εκκληση της Ακρόπολης», Κτίριο Κωστή Παλαμά
Ακαδημίας 48 & Σίνα - τηλ. 3635.444

The Peace Boat often visits Greece